A Full-Length Play

Mixed Nuts

By

SIMON J. DONOGHUE
&
NANCY MANERA

THE DRAMATIC PUBLISHING COMPANY

MIXED NUTS

A Full-Length Play

for Three Men, Five Women

CHARACTERS

EDNA. . . . . the landlady

MICHAEL CALDWELL . . . . an aspiring writer

MARSHALL RYAN . . . . another tenant, most often a vegetable

MIKE . . . . .Michael's other self

MRS. CALDWELL . . . . Michael's mother

TANYA ROMANOV . . . . a Russian dancer

PHIL DELLA VECCHIA . . . . .an aspiring actress

HEATHER. . . . . a model

TIME: Next Summer
PLACE: New York City

3

ACT ONE

SCENE: Apartment Five-C, the Adolph Zuckerman Home for Artistes.

AT RISE OF CURTAIN: EDNA, in bathrobe, fuzzy slippers and curlers, and MICHAEL, in his best suit and carrying two suitcases and a typewriter case, enter.

EDNA. Like I said before, the pay phone in the hall is for everyone on this floor, so try not to hog it. The last super put a long extension cord on the thing, so you can carry it in here if you need to talk private. (She gestures toward the kitchen area.) The sink is over there. You'll only get hot water from that faucet. If you want cold, you put it in the refrigerator.
MICHAEL. What's the chair by the refrigerator door for?
EDNA. It don't close without help, honey. Your stove is gas. Be careful with the controls, okay? The last tenant in this apartment was a model. Beautiful girl, just beautiful. But she kept fiddlin' with those controls. She ain't working anymore. The last I heard, they were still pickin' up scorched ears on Sixty-Seventh Street.
MICHAEL. That's awful!

EDNA. It's also not true. You're from out of town, aren't you, dearie?

MICHAEL (embarrassed). Can you tell?

EDNA. Only when you open your mouth. Whereabouts?

MICHAEL (moving about the apartment, checking it out). I'm from Dayton.

EDNA. Where's that?

MICHAEL. Ohio.

EDNA. Oh, Ohio. (She thinks a moment.) That's out west somewhere, ain't it?

MICHAEL (abstractedly). Go to St. Louis and take a right. You can't miss it.

EDNA. I ain't been out of this city in fifty-four years. I should start now?

MICHAEL. Never mind. (To the audience.) That's what I love about New Yorkers. In the three days that I've been here, I've noticed they are unable to imagine God created anything west of New Jersey.

EDNA. Look, sport, time is money and I ain't got all day. So what's it gonna be? You want the apartment or not?

MICHAEL. I don't know yet. What's the rent on this place?

EDNA. One hundred a week. First two weeks up front.

MICHAEL (incredulously). For *this*?

EDNA. Take it or leave it, ace. I got 'em lined up in the street waiting for an apartment in this place. Make up your mind. (MICHAEL pulls money from his wallet and hands it to EDNA. She counts it.) Thanks. Well, she's all yours. I'll have a lease for you in the morning. (She starts to leave, then turns back.) And remember, don't you be fiddlin' with that stove. You got any problems, call me or the mister and we'll take care of them for you. But don't call before noon, or after six, and *never* call on weekends. We go to my sister Tootie's place up in the Bronx. Oh, and I almost forgot. Welcome to the Adolph

Zuckerman Home for Artists.

MICHAEL. Artistes.

EDNA. What?

MICHAEL. The sign on the building says *artistes*, not artists.

EDNA. Whatever makes you happy, kid. (She starts to leave.)

MICHAEL (hastily). You see, that's what attracted me to the place. I'm in the arts. Or trying to be, anyway. Are there a lot of people like me living in this building?

EDNA (folding her arms). Yeah. Glenda Jackson, she lives down the hall. And of course, Steve and Eydie keep an apartment in the building for when they're in town. On the first floor, you got your singers. Barbra Streisand, Frank Sinatra and Beverly Sills.

MICHAEL. Sorry. I was just curious.

EDNA. Yeah, sure. By the way, Mr. Artiste, what is it you do?

MICHAEL. Oh, I'm a writer. I mean I'm going to be. A writer.

EDNA. Trying to convince yourself? What do you do, write those dirty books? I'm warning you, I don't want any perverts mucking around in my building.

MICHAEL. Gee, no, I never . . .

EDNA. Because I run a clean place. (She spots a cockroach on the floor and stomps on it, then exits. MICHAEL waits until he is sure EDNA has gone, then tears off the suit coat and tie. He does an impromptu victory dance, throws the typewriter case on the desk and the suitcases on the sofa. From one of the cases, he fishes out a framed photograph of his mother which he places on one of the endtables. He looks at it momentarily, then carefully turns the photo face down. As he continues to unpack, a bloodcurdling scream is heard from upstairs. Startled, he fumbles with his things as they drop all over the floor. He begins to pick them up and the scream is heard again. This time he runs to the door and throws it open.)

(MARSHALL, a man dressed as an olive, stands in the doorway, poised to knock.)

MARSHALL. Listen, man, could you do me a favor and zip me up? It's in the back, near the pimento line. (He turns around and MICHAEL mechanically zips him up while he tries to look out into the hall. All of a sudden it dawns on MICHAEL that MARSHALL is dressed like a vegetable and he does a double-take. MARSHALL walks into the apartment and surveys it with undisguised curiosity.) Thanks. You're the new kid on the block, right? My name's Marshall. Marshall Ryan. But don't get too used to it. I'n thinking of changing it to something with a little more pizzazz. Do you mind if I come in?

MICHAEL. Uh, no, but . . .

MARSHALL (perching on the arm of the couch). I know just what you're thinking. You're wondering why you let an olive into your apartment, right? I'm an actor. I'm doing a kind of street theatre piece this afternoon down in Times Square. I get to jump into a giant martini glass on the top of the Allied Chemical Building. We're plugging a new brand of gin. Pretty original idea, don't you think?

MICHAEL. Did you just hear a scream?

MARSHALL (shrugging). Yeah. It was nothing. Anyway, I'm getting two hundred dollars for it. And a case of the gin. Not that I put that kind of poison into my system, but I can probably hustle the stuff for a few bucks. By the way, do you drink gin?

MICHAEL. How can you be sure the scream was nothing?

MARSHALL. Don't lose your pants over it! It was only Tanya. She's a free-lance ballerina. Lives upstairs. Screaming is part of her therapy. The rumor mill around the mailboxes has it she's recovering from a fling with Baryshnikov.

MICHAEL. *Mikhail* Baryshnikov?

MARSHALL (with a look). No, *Fred* Baryshnikov. Listen, did Edna tell you the famous story about the model's ear?

MICHAEL. She may have mentioned it in passing. What kind of therapy is screaming at the top of your lungs?

MARSHALL. Primal. You know, you try to revert to your most primitive emotions. Screaming, punching, all that jazz. It was a lot easier on all of us when Tanya was into transcendental meditation. Personally, I think she just likes to scream and the therapy gives her an excuse to cut loose. (He peers into Michael's open suitcase.) Have you got anything to eat? (He takes an apple out of the suitcase.) Can I eat this?

MICHAEL (starting to unpack again). Sure. It might be a little mealy, though. I bought it before I left home.

MARSHALL. No problem, amigo. When you're a professional scrounger, you learn to eat anything. (He moves to the desk and sits on top of it.) So, you still haven't said what you think of the costume and . . . by the way, I don't think I caught your name.

MICHAEL. I'm Michael Caldwell. (He and MARSHALL shake hands.) And you look like an olive.

MARSHALL. Great. But you know what? In here . . . (He indicates his heart.) . . . I don't *feel* like an olive. No joke. See, I did two years with Strasberg and it took. I mean, it really took. Method acting had me becoming any part I played. When your specialty is fruit and vegetables, that has definite disadvantages. Once I landed a part as one of the Fruit of the Loom gang in those commercials for underwear. You know the ones I mean? Anyway, for three weeks I had the mentality and social disposition of a Concord grape. This olive thing is the first time I've let myself play a vegetable in a year, but I think I'm gonna be able to handle it. For two hundred bucks, I can *make* myself handle it.

MICHAEL. Let me get this straight. Your specialty as an actor is playing vegetables?

MARSHALL (matter-of-factly). And fruit. It's not easy getting legitimate work. I do a lot of commercials. And there was a real gap for this kind of stuff. Someone had to fill it. It pays, and that's the main thing. Just get into town?

MICHAEL. About three days ago. I've been staying over at the Chelsea Hotel while I looked for an apartment. (He looks around.) This isn't exactly what I had in mind. I guess it does have some character, though.

MARSHALL. It also has some bugs. There are cockroaches in my apartment that can pull up chairs and eat with me. Where did you come from?

MICHAEL. Ohio. (He goes into the kitchen to test the sink.)

MARSHALL. I'm from Portland. I lived in L. A. for a year but couldn't take it. Too many oddballs. And the next time I'm *that* laid back, I want to be dead. You were lucky to get this place because the rent is so low.

MICHAEL. I don't think four hundred dollars a month is so low.

MARSHALL. That's because you're still operating on Ohio prices. See the skyscrapers out there? This is Manhattan. Four hundred bucks gets you a closet in most of those buildings.

MICHAEL. I guess you're right. Mind if I clear the desk? (MARSHALL moves to the couch.) When did you come to New York?

MARSHALL. Five years ago. It wasn't exactly by choice. I landed a part in a road company of *Here's Broadway*.

MICHAEL. Never heard of it.

MARSHALL. You and everybody else. It died a dismal death in Trenton and we were all stranded. New York seemed the logical solution. (MICHAEL takes the typewriter out of the case and sets it on the desk.) Hey, are you a writer or something like that?

MICHAEL. That's what I'm here to find out. (There is another scream from upstairs.)

MARSHALL. Ooops, there goes lungs. (He checks his watch.)

Hum, about time for the mail. I've got to get to it before Tanya does. Where she comes from, reading other people's mail is the national sport. It's been nice meeting you, Michael. I'm downstairs in Four-A, if you should need anything. See you later. (He exits.)

MICHAEL (calling after MARSHALL). Good luck with the jump! (To the audience.) And people say there are a lot of weirdos in New York City.

(MIKE comes through the door, suitcase in hand. He is dressed exactly like MICHAEL.)

MIKE. Are we calling what just passed me in the hall normal?

MICHAEL. For Pete's sake, will you let me introduce *myself* before *you* arrive on the scene? (To the audience.) As you may have heard, my name is Michael Caldwell. Michael Stoddard Caldwell, to be more precise.

MIKE (to the audience). Precision is one of his most annoying traits. I've been working on it for years.

MICHAEL. I thought I left you back in Dayton.

MIKE. Fat chance! (He settles down on the couch.)

MICHAEL. But one of my main reasons for leaving was to get away from you!

MIKE (with a look). Don't whine. I *hate* it when you whine. If it wasn't for me, you wouldn't be here.

MICHAEL. That's not true!

MIKE (calmly). Sure it is. And you know it. (To the audience.) I get stuck with all the dirty work.

MICHAEL. You're making me feel like a schizophrenic!

MIKE (exasperated). Grow up! Everybody has another side to them. The only difference is, yours talks back.

MICHAEL. A lot!

MIKE (reasonably). Not as much as I could, if you'd only let

me. Face it, you *need* me. I had to drag you to the train
station. If I hadn't put my foot down, you'd still be writing
obituaries for the *Dayton Press*.

MICHAEL (sulking). It was better than working for Dad.

MIKE. The man is a mortician! What's the difference! (He
calms down.) Don't you want to write about the living for a
change?

MICHAEL. I'm just scared, that's all. What if I don't have the
talent?

MIKE. I'm telling you, you've got to work on your self-image.
Where's the bottle?

MICHAEL. What bottle?

MIKE. Will you knock it off! I helped you sneak it into the
suitcase, remember? (He digs into Michael's suitcase until he
finds a bottle of Scotch. He leans back on the couch, props
the bottle on his knee, and lets out a sigh of satisfaction.) Ah,
bliss. It's too bad Mom isn't around to see her little boy and
demon rum in action.

(MRS. CALDWELL, Michael's mother, floats out from the bathroom. Well-dressed and middle-aged, she has a face that would
stop the average charging Bengal tiger.)

MRS. CALDWELL. That's right. Drink. Twist the knife in my
heart.

MICHAEL (betraying no surprise at the sight of her). Mother.
I'm over twenty-one. And one drink isn't going to put me
under the table.

MRS. CALDWELL. It has before, remember?

MICHAEL. No.

MIKE. Yes.

MICHAEL. When? What is she talking about?

MIKE. Uncle Bud's wedding. We got so bombed, we puked on

the man's wedding cake.

MICHAEL (outraged). I was six years old!

MIKE. So? Even at that age, we should have known Drambuie and Fresca don't cut it.

MRS. CALDWELL. There. You see? If you won't listen to me, listen to him. (She scrutinizes MIKE.) Whoever he is.

MICHAEL. This isn't New York — it's the Twilight Zone! (To MRS. CALDWELL.) What do you mean, whoever he is? He's *me*!

MRS. CALDWELL (unruffled). Why are you yelling at me, young man. None of this is *my* fault.

MIKE. She's right. We are *your* fantasy.

MICHAEL. I don't believe this. My own imagination is ganging up on me!

MIKE. Your guilt must be working overtime.

MICHAEL. I don't see why. (MRS. CALDWELL moves around the apartment and checks for dust.) It's not like I did anything wrong. I told her where I was going, didn't I? (To the audience.) I really did! Watch. (To MRS. CALDWELL.) Mother, I love you and Dad very much, and I don't want you to worry. But I have to go to New York. I do. It's for the best. A big city environment will help me to grow as a writer. (To the audience.) That's rational, isn't it?

MIKE. Sure is. It would have worked if Mom and Dad were rational.

MICHAEL. It did work. (A pause.) I think.

MIKE. Think again. (To the audience.) Michael's mother has a slightly different version of how that scene just went. This is how it looked from *her* side. (He swaggers over and grabs MRS. CALDWELL by her coat lapel.) Mom, I'm going to New York whether you like it or not. I want to mistreat small animals and eat lots of Indonesian food! (He grabs her other lapel.) I want to shoplift! And after that, I want to die a bum in the gutter,

having disgraced the Caldwell family name and wasted my life!
(He lets MRS. CALDWELL go, thoroughly pleased with himself.)

MRS. CALDWELL (hysterically). Oh, my God! Oh, my God!
(She runs out of the room through the bathroom door.)

MIKE (to MICHAEL). Are you happy? You just broke the
heart of the woman who gave you life! (He punches MICHAEL
in the arm and exits into the bedroom.)

MICHAEL (aghast). But *I* didn't! *You* did — that never
happened — this is confusing! (There is a knock at the door.)
Who is it?

TANYA (from offstage, in a heavy Russian accent). Is Tanya
Romanov, neighbor from upstairs.

MICHAEL (opening the door). Come on in.

(TANYA barges in, dressed in a cross between high elegance and
a warm-up outfit.)

TANYA. I am meeting Marshall by mailbox. He say to meet
Misha Caldwell is greatest pleasure of day. Tanya decide to
take advice of little olive. Can Tanya sit, pliss? (Her seating
movement on the couch is a symphony of graceful flutters.
MICHAEL appears a little stunned before the onslaught.)

MICHAEL. What are you doing?

TANYA (shrugging modestly). Is gift. (She looks MICHAEL
over.) Edna is right. You *are* little fox. So from where you
are?

MICHAEL (obviously tired of this particular topic). Dayton.

TANYA. Ohio! Tanya once dance the Swan in Ohio. Perhaps
you are lucky enough to see her, yes?

MICHAEL. I'm afraid not.

TANYA. Is okay. Audience was rubes anyways. In middle of
big dying scene, after I am being shot by wicked hunter, old

lady in third row with blue hair say Tanya twinkle on tippytoe. (She bellows.) Tanya does not *twinkle*! She *lives* to dance! It is her life!

MICHAEL. I can see that.

TANYA.   You are perceptive little shvipsik, Misha Caldwell. (She stands and stretches.) Tanya is sitting too long. Is bad for body fluids one needs to dance. She must shake them free! (She emits a full-throated scream.)

MICHAEL. Stop that! Do you want to get me thrown out of the apartment?

TANYA (heartily). Not to worry, Misha! Edna, the landlady, she scream with Tanya. *Everyone* scream with Tanya! Come, little malenkaia! (She grabs MICHAEL by the arms and places him next to herself. MICHAEL stands sheepishly as TANYA strikes a ballet pose.)

MICHAEL. I don't think —

TANYA (interrupting). Misha! Listen to Tanya! Legs apart, pliss.   (MICHAEL does not move.)   Legs *apart*, pliss! (MICHAEL spreads his legs apart.) Now. First, we are breathing deeply. (She shuts her eyes and breathes in a bushel of air.) Tanya cannot *hear* you!

MICHAEL (holding his breath). I'm breathing! I'm breathing!

TANYA. Now, let out. (BOTH deflate.) Misha, you are not being dancer? (He shakes his head.) Then for why you are coming to Big Apple?

MICHAEL (heading for the couch). To write. I'm a writer.

TANYA (grabbing MICHAEL again). Not so fast, bubbaleh! We haven't finished our routine! Shoulders back!

MICHAEL. Please, Miss Romanov, I don't want to . . .

TANYA (oblivious). Follow Tanya! (She stretches her arms apart and begins to touch her toes, left hand to right toe, right hand to left toe, etc.) And one and two and one and two and one and two and *count with Tanya* and one and two and . . .

MICHAEL (mumbling and doing the routine). . . . and one and two and one and two . . .

TANYA. Hokay, *stop*! (MICHAEL is pooped.) So you are writer?

MICHAEL. Yeah. (He heads for the couch and TANYA grabs him again.)

TANYA. What you write about?

MICHAEL (exhausted). Fiction, mostly.

TANYA. I don't know him. Arms out! (She begins waist twists.) And one and two and two and one and two. You know, Misha, you are lucky to be living downstairs from Tanya.

MICHAEL (keeping pace). How's that?

TANYA. You will be having chance to write about one of greatest dancers of all time.

MICHAEL (stopping as he is struck by the thought). Hey, that's right. Marshall told me you knew Baryshnikov. Do you think I could meet him sometime? He'd make a great —

TANYA (interrupting, furiously). How dare you speak of this swine in the presence of Tanya? (She speeds up the exercises.) Ungrateful Cossack! Tossing Tanya aside like he do to take up with many American schnookniks! You believe he do this to me? You believe? (She utters a primal scream.) *Stop*! (She composes herself.) Misha, Tanya did not mean him for your story.

MICHAEL (collapsing on the couch). Who then?

TANYA (sitting next to MICHAEL). You are *slow*, Yankee Doodle. Tanya means Tanya, of course.

MICHAEL. Oh?

TANYA. Let Tanya tell you a little of herself and then you will understand, da?

MICHAEL (sliding down the couch to get away from TANYA). That's okay. I mean, I don't want to keep you from anything that you might have to do.

TANYA. Must Tanya scream to get you to listen?

MICHAEL. On the other hand, I'm sure it's a fascinating story.

TANYA. Tanya has had quite interesting a life, beginning of course with her birth in Vladivostock. It is there my parents were in tragic exile. (She cries, then notices MICHAEL is not writing anything down and changes her mood.) Shouldn't you be taking for yourself some *notes*?

MICHAEL. No. I have a very good memory. Why are your parents in exile?

TANYA. They are not in exile no more. They are dying in salt mines ten years ago. Is wery sad.

MICHAEL. Were they political prisoners?

TANYA. Misha, my last name is Romanov. What *you* think?

MICHAEL. Wait a minute here. Are you trying to tell me that you're related to the Russian Imperial family?

TANYA. Not merely related, baboochnik. There is excellent possibility that Tanya is rightful Tsarina of all the Russians.

MICHAEL. And you're living in *this* building?

TANYA. It does not mean as much as it used to. But Tanya is happy child, dancing and singing in the streets of Vladivostok. Only when she is becoming twelve years old a gypsy fortune teller sees terrible danger for her. She see K.G.B. in her crystal ball, and they are chasing me across frozen tundra. Tanya has only one choice. She must take it on the lam, as Mr. James Cagney say in your American cinema films. For four years, I am underground. I suffer horribly. Finally, I get false papers and hide out with tiny Lithuanian dance company. It is there that her grace, her balance, enable Tanya to become prima ballerina of Lithuania. And, finally, when dance company is inwited to America, Tanya make up her mind. She must become . . . defective. (MICHAEL does a take.) It was wery hard decision. Only sight of tenth floor Bloomingdale's conwince her that America really *is* land of opportunity, true freedom, and many, *many* nice clothes.

MICHAEL. So how'd you do it?

TANYA. On afternoon of final performance, I run away. For two weeks, I hide out in American movie house. Is by watching old cinema films that Tanya learn the language of this country. Listen! "You dirty rat! I am giving it to you like you give it to my sister!" You know that cinema film? Nyet? How about this? "I could be being somebody. I could be being big contender, instead of being big bum, which is what I am being." Mr. Marlon Brando say that in *On The Waterfront*. So now, Misha, you are knowing a little of Tanya. Is interesting stuff, nyet?

MICHAEL. Nyet. I mean, yes. It is!

TANYA. Good. Then enough small talk. (She moves in on MICHAEL.)

MICHAEL (moving over and pushing TANYA off). Hey, wait a minute!

TANYA. Something wrong?

MICHAEL. Yes, something is wrong!

TANYA. Are you not having natural male desires?

MICHAEL. Well . . . sure, but . . .

TANYA. Good. (She goes for MICHAEL again.)

MICHAEL. Will you please hold it for a second?

TANYA. What now, Misha? Tanya is quickly losing mood.

MICHAEL. It's just that I barely know you.

TANYA. Bare? Why you not say so in first place? (She goes for Michael's shirt.)

MICHAEL (leaping off the couch). Stop! Now is just not a good time to get to . . . know one another. After all, I just got in from Dayton and . . . (He fakes a yawn.) . . . I'm really kind of tired, if you know what I mean.

TANYA (the light dawning after a long pause). Oh! Tanya understand! Little Misha wants to save up all energy before he make big move! How *cute* you are! (She heads for the door.) Another time, then, my hot-blooded one. Tanya go now. Is time to talk to plants anyways. Kiss-kiss! (She exits.)

MICHAEL. I don't know how much more of this I can take.

(MIKE enters from the bathroom.)

MIKE. I thought she was a riot. Nijinsky in drag.

MICHAEL. Go away.

MIKE. This is beginning to look like a fun place to live. (He sits.) And you certainly aren't going to lack for something to write about. That chick alone is a guaranteed novel.

MICHAEL. What is that supposed to mean?

MIKE. Do I have to spell it out for you? This place! This environment! It's perfect. You don't even have to make anything up. In fact, you're not good enough to make up this stuff. I wonder what other nutburgers live in this joint?

MICHAEL. I hope I don't have to find out this afternoon. I'm beat.

MIKE. Don't be ridiculous. Get some paper in that typewriter and put this down before you forget it. (There is another primal scream from Tanya's apartment.)

MICHAEL (looking up). I don't think she'll slip my mind. Alright, let me think about it. (He goes into the bathroom and shuts the door.)

MIKE. *You* think about it, sportin' life. My mind is made up. This is going to be the story of the year! (He sits at the desk and starts to type. The lights fade to black.)

(It is one week later and MICHAEL has left his mark on the apartment. It looks lived in, to say the least. MICHAEL is at his desk, typing, as the lights come up. After a few seconds, there is a scream from Tanya's apartment.)

MICHAEL (checking his watch). Two-thirty already? (He moves to the couch and takes a bite from a half-eaten sandwich on the coffee table.)

(MRS. CALDWELL appears in the bathroom doorway.)

MRS. CALDWELL. Look what he's eating! What is that?

MICHAEL (with his mouth full). Chef-Boy-Ar-Dee ravioli on white bread. It's delicious.

MRS. CALDWELL (moving into the room). Only a week in New York and you're living like this? Where did we go wrong?

MICHAEL. Probably with the Montessori school.

MRS. CALDWELL. Don't smart-mouth *me*, young man. That school at least stressed responsibility. (She looks around the room.) And neatness. When did you become allergic to Pine Sol?

MICHAEL. What difference does it make how the place looks? The important thing is that I'm finally getting some work done. You know, that reminds me. I've been here a week and you and Father still haven't found me.

MRS. CALDWELL. We've been working on rectifying *that* situation. The detective agency we hired has tracked you down. (The hall phone rings.) In fact, I think that's your father now. Answer the phone.

MICHAEL. You hired a detective agency?

MRS. CALDWELL. Three. Two in Dayton and one in New York. Will you *please* answer the phone? (She exits through the bathroom. There is a knock on the door and MICHAEL goes to answer it.)

(MICHAEL opens the door to find PHILOMENA DELLA VECCHIA standing in the doorway. She is dressed in a bath-robe and holds the phone receiver in her hand. Intelligent and interesting-looking, she is more than slightly annoyed.)

PHIL. Are you by any chance Michael Caldwell?

MICHAEL. That's right.

PHIL. Por vous. (She hands MICHAEL the phone and stalks into his apartment.)

MICHAEL (into the receiver). Hello? (Stricken.) Hello, Father.

PHIL. Got any coffee in this dump?

MICHAEL (covering the mouthpiece). Try the shelf over the sink. (PHIL walks over to the kitchen area and begins to open the cabinets while MICHAEL returns to the phone.) Yes, Father . . . Father, if you would just let me explain . . .

PHIL. I mean *real* coffee. (She holds up a jar.) This is Sanka.

MICHAEL (to PHIL). All I've got. (Into the phone.) Yes, Father. No, sir, there's no one else here. (PHIL gives MICHAEL a look.) Yes . . . no, sir, I didn't mean to break Mother's heart. How did you find me? No, sir, I didn't mean to upset you either. Where I'm living? Oh, it's great, just great. (There is another scream from upstairs.) That? Nothing. It was a seagull. My apartment fronts on the East River. (PHIL wanders over and stands behind MICHAEL.) Father, I really can't talk now. I'm in the middle of a shower. (PHIL makes running water sounds into the receiver.) But I am alright. Yes. (PHIL goes back to the kitchen area and scrounges around for a pot. She finds one and fills it with water, then places it on the stove.) I'll talk to you soon. No, sir, not tonight. I was thinking more like tomorrow or the end of the week. (There is an explosion through the receiver and MICHAEL winces.) Yes, sir. Tomorrow. My love to Mother. Goodbye, Father. (MICHAEL goes out into the hall to return the phone.)

(MICHAEL re-enters and goes to PHIL.)

MICHAEL. Sorry about that.

PHIL (at the typewriter, reading what MICHAEL has written). It's okay. Just try not to let it happen again. Are you really a writer or just kidding yourself?

MICHAEL. Who are you? And what are you doing in here, anyway?

PHIL. Excuse *me* for having a heart that's beating. I'm Phil Della Vecchia. I live down the hall. (Meaningfully.) Next to the *phone*?

MICHAEL. Oh, right. I'm sorry. I'm going to have one put in next week. (After a long pause, a little unnerved.) Gee, Della Vecchia. That's Italian, isn't it?

PHIL. No. Isn't it obvious? I'm a Viking.

MICHAEL. Phil is certainly an unusual name for a woman.

PHIL. Not if your first name is Philomena. And where I come from, Caldwell ain't exactly a run of the mill handle either.

MICHAEL (floundering). Are you sick or something?

PHIL. First impressions aren't your forte, are they?

MICHAEL. Look, I said I was sorry. But you *are* in your bathrobe and it *is* the middle of the afternoon. I thought maybe —

PHIL (interrupting). I apologize for not dressing for the occasion. If I'd known I was going to be playing answering service for you this afternoon, I would have put on something a little more uptown. (MICHAEL turns away.) Alright, I'm sorry. (The water boils. She goes over , takes it from the stove, and begins to make a cup of instant coffee.) It's just that I work nights and I don't usually get up 'til around five.

MICHAEL. What do you do, if you don't mind my asking?

PHIL. Milk?

MICHAEL. In the refrigerator.

PHIL. How original. (She gets the milk, pours it, puts it back in the refrigerator, then kicks the door shut.) I'm sorry again. Did you say something?

MICHAEL. I just asked what you did for a living.

PHIL (sitting). I'm an actress. I play Liesl in the Jones Beach Summer Theatre production of *The Sound of Music*.

MICHAEL. I don't remember the movie too well. Is that a good part?

PHIL (singing in a whiny voice). "I am sixteen going on thirty-two." It stinks, but it pays three hundred a week. Not that the money is enough to compensate for the thrill of acting at sea. Have you ever seen anything out there?

MICHAEL. No. I just got into –

PHIL (interrupting). Yeah, well, you haven't missed anything. Except maybe last night. All of the sets are floating barges, right? And these little tug boats push them on and off. So, last night, Morty – he's one of the guys who steers the tugs – good old Mort got just a bit high and accidentally rammed the set during the second act. It was awful. Everywhere you looked there were drowning nuns trying to pull themselves in with their rosary beads. (She notices Michael's sandwich.) What was that before it died?

MICHAEL. My lunch.

PHIL (inspecting it). Cheese ravioli on white bread? You should try the meat ravioli. It's better. I'm an ethnic. Trust me. So how long have you been writing?

MICHAEL. Several years.

PHIL. Marshall told me you were from the midwest somewhere. What did you do, come to New York to find your fame and fortune? (In a deep voice.) "There are ten million stories in the Naked City. This is one of them." (She realizes that MICHAEL is not laughing.) Oh, no! You *did*, didn't you! Well, let's take a look. (She walks over to the typewriter and reads aloud. MICHAEL mouths the words as she says them.) "The man came into the cafe. It was a dirty cafe. The dirt was everywhere. The grime filled his nostrils with the stench of despair and lost hopes." You've got *your* nerve, buster!

MICHAEL. What do you mean?

PHIL. Hasn't anyone clued you in to the big secret? The one person who best illustrates the simplicity of the Hemingway style is Papa himself!

MICHAEL. You don't understand! It's supposed to be like that. See, I'm entering this literary contest.

PHIL. When did they start giving a Pulitzer Prize for unoriginality?

MICHAEL. It's the Harry's American Bar and Grill Write-Like-Hemingway Contest. The name comes from a bar Hemingway used to go to in Italy.

PHIL. Yeah? What do you get for winning?

MICHAEL. They fly you to Florence for a meal at Harry's.

PHIL. Just you?

MICHAEL. Well, no, come to think of it. They give you an extra ticket for a friend.

PHIL. This little piece will never make it. You did say Florence, Italy?

MICHAEL. Yeah.

PHIL. I've always wanted to go to Italy. (She rips the sheet of paper from the typewriter.) Sit down and write what I tell you. (MICHAEL sits down. PHIL paces for a moment.) "The sun glinted off the snows of Kilamanjaro as the hunter left camp. The sun was also rising as he left. Far in the distance, the hunter could see an old man on the sea."

MICHAEL. Gee, you're pretty literate.

PHIL. What is *that* supposed to mean?

MICHAEL. Well, you know what they say about actors. That they're kind of, uh, flighty.

PHIL. And all Orientals carry cameras. For your information, I have a Master's in English Lit from Columbia.

MICHAEL (impressed). Oh?

PHIL (shrugging). I really don't. But I could have. I dated a professor in the English department for a year. When it blew up, I dumped him but stole his books.

MICHAEL. Were you born in New York?

PHIL. Over in Brooklyn. Bay Ridge.

MICHAEL. Bay Ridge. That sounds pretty.

PHIL. It's okay. My family is still there. The Italian Waltons of Bath Avenue.

MICHAEL. Do you have a large family?

PHIL. Not by our standards, but probably to you we're an emerging nation. Seven kids. And, of course, my grandparents live with us. And my cousin Angela, who is thirty-two and still not married, God help her. Oh, yeah, and Uncle Cheech. He used to drive for Al Capone. Seriously. The man is seventy-eight years old and still has an unnatural fear of cement. What's your tribe like?

MICHAEL. Not nearly as colorful. They live in Dayton. Mother is . . . middle-aged.

PHIL. Sounds like a real madcap.

MICHAEL. And my father once had a letter published in *Time* magazine.

PHIL. Brothers and sisters?

MICHAEL. No. I'm an only child.

PHIL. Are you the last of the red-hot Caldwells? Does the fate of the family name rest on *your* frail shoulders?

MICHAEL. No. My Uncle Bud and Aunt Allison have a couple of kids. Their son Biff is about sixteen.

PHIL. *Biff?* (She shows off.) Oh, as in Willy-Loman-*Death-of-a-Salesman* Biff?

MICHAEL. Biff as in my grandfather, Michael Bifferton Caldwell the third.

PHIL. I've never known anyone who had a real number attached to his name. Except Uncle Cheech. But he got his at Sing-Sing.

You know, against my better judgment, I'm suddenly finding your *Teen Beat* good looks minimally attractive.

MICHAEL. Huh?

PHIL. Read my lips. I . . . like . . . you. How about the two of us grabbing some breakfast somewhere?

MICHAEL. Uh, well . . .

PHIL (setting down her coffee). Hey, if you can't make it, it's okay.

MICHAEL. I'd really better not. I have a few things to get finished up here. But thanks.

PHIL. Sure, any time. (She exits. After a beat, there is a knock on the door.)

(MICHAEL opens the door and finds PHIL again.)

PHIL. Why not?

MICHAEL. What?

PHIL. Why don't you want to eat with me? (She walks into the apartment.) What is so pressing *here* that you can't come? Or is it . . . no, it couldn't be . . . *me*? I know that's ridiculous, right? (A pause.) Right? So what is it? Oh, I get it. You've just come in from Indiana.

MICHAEL. Ohio!

PHIL. Regardless. Anyway, you're standing there thinking unto your own sweet self, "Hey, wait a *minute*. Here I am in New York City and an unbelievable knockout of a girl enters my place and invites *me* to breakfast. If only the guys at Dayton High could see me now." But you think, "Gee" — like you do so well — "Gee, if I go, I'll only make a fool of myself being the unslick zero that I am. I'll wait until I get better acquainted with New York *and* her, and then I'll take her someplace that will compliment her certain je ne ce quois, her understated elegance." Am I right, Michael?

MICHAEL. I don't think —

PHIL (interrupting). Because if I'm not, then the only other reason is that you're scared of me. You've just come to New York. A stranger enters your apartment with nothing but a phone, a bathrobe and a lot of smart remarks. You think I'm one of those psychopaths you read about in those "New York — The World's Cesspool" articles. That I won't take you to breakfast but club you to death in some subway bathroom with a curling iron. So to put your midwestern mind at ease, I'll give you a capsulized version of the internationally famous "Get To Know Philomena Della Vecchia Course in Ten Easy Lessons." Sit down. (MICHAEL sits.) Now then. Likes and dislikes. I like Ingrid Bergman movies, trenchcoats, following celebrities around New York and chocolate. I think I like chocolate the best. My pet peeves are steak, Olivia Newton-John — all that blond hair and all those blue eyes — and people who label everything as Freudian. Usually they're the same ones who say garbage like "Have a nice day!" and "We're not relating." That's great because then I only have to avoid one large group of people. Saves energy. End of sermonette. Now can we please go *eat*?

MICHAEL (bemused). Do you always talk this much?

PHIL (checking an imaginary watch). Going once, going twice . . .

MICHAEL (quickly). Okay, okay. And breakfast is on me.

PHIL. I thought *that* was understood. And because you're such a nice guy, I'm going to stick you front and center for tonight's performance.

MICHAEL. Gee, that would be swell.

PHIL (in wonder). "Gee, that would be swell?" (A pause while she looks blankly at MICHAEL.) Who *are* you? Andy Hardy? (As BOTH exit.) You get your dad's barn and I'll get the costumes. Let's put on a show! (The lights dim quickly as the apartment door closes.)

(It is three-thirty a.m , the following day. As the lights come up,
    PHIL and MICHAEL enter the apartment. PHIL is obviously
    agitated and her hair is damp.)

PHIL. This is great, really great! At seven o'clock this evening, I
    was an actress. Now I'm just another girl shafted by Marlo
    Thomas.
MICHAEL (befogged). What? (He removes his sports coat.)
PHIL. Marlo Thomas! Mrs. Phil Donahue! Don't you remember
    That Girl? I'd like to know how many girls came to New York
    and bagged a boffo apartment *and* the man of their dreams all
    on the same day! And we're not talking losers here! Not for
    Little Miss Perfect! She bags the editor of some fancy-
    schmantzy magazine who doesn't even mind the fact that the
    bimbo never got a job!
MICHAEL. What are you talking about?
PHIL. *I don't know*! (She sits on the couch.) All I know is that
    I'm unemployed. Again. This is all Morty's fault. After last
    night, they never should have let him back on tug duty.
MICHAEL (moving toward the kitchen area). You have to admit,
    it was pretty funny. Do you want some coffee?
PHIL. Funny? When the light bank blew and the Alps caught
    fire, it looked like Pearl Harbor out there! How many actors
    do *you* know who can say that their last play sank and can
    mean it literally? This kind of thing travels fast, too. By
    morning, it's going to be all over the place, and my life as an
    actor will be over. I will never work again. Finito. Kaputski.
    Not until I am old and decrepit will someone hire me. (She
    speaks tragically.) "It is an ancient actress and she stoppeth
    one of three . . ."
MICHAEL (laughing). Don't be so dramatic. I don't think any-
    one really noticed. You all covered well.
PHIL. Oh, right. They probably thought the Coast Guard was

part of the chorus. Can't you get it through your head that my meal ticket just drowned?

MICHAEL. Something else will come up. You'll see.

PHIL (mimicing MICHAEL). "Something else will come up." Look, Michael, the first thing you learn in the theatre is that nothing just comes *up*. Oh, God. This means I have to start making rounds in the morning.

MICHAEL. Rounds?

PHIL. Rounds. Auditions. Self-humiliation of the highest order. Well, at least it's June. They'll be casting for the fall. Listen, I'm too depressed to discuss this right now. Where's that coffee? (MICHAEL prepares the coffee.) I knew it. I just knew it. This is the famous curse of the Della Vecchias in action. Seven years ago, my grandmother stood in the middle of the kitchen and ritually cursed me for refusing to marry Tony Mancini. It finally paid off tonight.

MICHAEL (handing PHIL a cup of coffee). Who's Tony Mancini?

PHIL. This guy I dated in high school. My family had really high hopes, *if* you know what I mean. (She gestures the pulling on of a wedding ring.) At the time, there was a little concern about my winding up another cousin Angela. They were right! I was an idiot not to take Tony up on his offer. At least he's got a steady job these days.

MICHAEL. C.P.A.?

PHIL. Nah, he's a priest. (A pause.) I ought to give him a call. Maybe it's still not too late. (She gazes moodily into her cup.)

MICHAEL (trying to pull PHIL out of her mood). I was pretty serious about a girl once.

PHIL (flatly). Am I to be spared *nothing* on this, my night of nights? Now it's the details of hot monkey love in Dayton! What did you do, take her to proms?

MICHAEL (a bit miffed). Look, Phil, I'm only trying to take your mind off everything!

PHIL (giving in). Okay, *tell* me about her!

MICHAEL. Never mind, now!

PHIL. No, really. Come on. (She is bored.) I'm *dying* to know. What was her name?

MICHAEL. Cindy Evans. (He pauses, slightly embarrassed. PHIL makes a gesture of pulling it out of MICHAEL.) She had blond hair and blue eyes.

PHIL. I bet she wore her hair in a pony tail and was perpetually tanned.

MICHAEL. How did you know that?

PHIL. Lucky guess. Does this get any better?

MICHAEL. Yeah. (He pauses, then speaks unwillingly.) We were pretty involved.

PHIL. How involved?

MICHAEL. We were kind of . . . engaged.

PHIL. Engaged! (She looks MICHAEL over.) Still waters *do* run deep! For how long?

MICHAEL (even more embarrassed). For all I know, we still are. Cindy doesn't exactly know I'm in New York.

PHIL. You jilted a girl named Cindy who wears a pony tail? What kind of animals do they breed in Ohio? The poor little twit. She's probably back in Dayton working on a terminal case of heartache! I mean, who's she gonna get to take her to the country club dance this Saturday night? (More seriously.) Anyway, were you in love with her?

MICHAEL. I asked her to marry me.

PHIL. So what happened?

MICHAEL (slowly). I'm not sure. It wasn't anything she did. And it wasn't anything she didn't do. I guess the problem is . . . me. But I don't really know how to explain it. Cindy once told me . . .

PHIL. What?

MICHAEL. She once told me that when we kissed, she always felt that I wasn't there.

PHIL. Sounds like a charming girl.

MICHAEL. No, I knew what she meant. She was right. My heart wasn't in it. I can't explain it any better than that.

PHIL (shrugging). Don't try, then.

MICHAEL. You're the first person to say that. Thanks for understanding.

PHIL. I didn't say I understood. I just mean you don't owe *me* an explanation.

MICHAEL. I only hope she doesn't hate me. How would you feel if something like this happened to you? Would you hate the guy?

PHIL (considering). I'd never let it get that far. But if I ever did, I guess I'd be angry. Yeah, really angry. Anyway, what's the diff?

MICHAEL (sitting). After all, I'm here and she's there.

PHIL. And bullets don't travel that far.

MICHAEL. Were you in love with the guy you dated?

PHIL. Who, Eric? *He* told me I was, so what did I know? He was amazing, in a slimy sort of way. Feature this: he taught English at Columbia; he collected Oriental rugs; he had a beard, of course; there were suede elbow patches on every article of clothing he owned — including his pajamas — and there was a picture of Karl Marx on his office wall. The man wrote the book on academic stereotypes.

MICHAEL. If you thought he was so funny, then why did you go out with him?

PHIL. At the time, I was impressed with the image. When I was nineteen, things like suede elbow patches meant a lot. And Eric was the first man to talk to me as though I had a functioning mind. It turned out I did, and it was better than his. Let me give you one of the many examples. My agency once got me an audition for the Princess Leia part in *Star Wars*. God alone knows how.

MICHAEL. You're kidding! I loved that movie! I think I saw it five times!

PHIL. You would have loved it even more if it had been *me* in that rocket with Harrison Ford. But Eric talked me out of it. He said it was ridiculous for someone who was trying to get recognition as a serious actress to even consider a role like that. And I bought it, for which I am still kicking myself. That's not to say I would have been cast, but who knows? Stranger things have happened.

MICHAEL. What did you do after that?

PHIL. I wound up in a play down on Bleeker Street that Eric wrote. It was experimental, which is a theatrical euphemism for looney-tunes. I spent the first act sitting in a playpen repeating the word "ambivalence."

MICHAEL. Why?

PHIL. As God is my witness, I don't know. When I asked Eric, he said that "ambivalence" was a microscopic representation of the symbolic frustration of the blue collar worker, which meant that *he* didn't know either.

MICHAEL. Is that when you dumped him?

PHIL. I should have, but I felt so sorry for the guy when the play closed after one performance that I let it drag on. Then I found out that he was running around with some coed transfer from Bennington. Eric claimed that she understood him — and his work — on a more meaningful level than I was ever capable of achieving. And *that's* when I dumped him.

MICHAEL. I'm sorry.

PHIL. C'est la vie. (A pause.) So how's the writing going? I know you've only been here a week, but have you sold anything yet?

MICHAEL (ruefully). I wish.

PHIL. Then if you don't mind my asking, how are you support-
ing yourself? Running a numbers racket out of this place?

MICHAEL. I cashed in the trust fund my grandfather left me the
day I came to New York. It should be enough to get me
through the winter. After that, I don't know what I'll do for
money.

PHIL (goggling at MICHAEL). What are you moaning about?
A *trust* fund? All my grandfather ever gave me was his union
card!

MICHAEL. Phil, if you need some help, I can loan you enough
to . . .

PHIL. Oh, God, Michael, I've got some savings. I'm just kvetch-
ing. It's a hobby. Some people collect glass, I kvetch. I know
I'm good at it, but don't take it seriously. Don't people ever
kvetch about money where you come from?

MICHAEL. Kvetch?

PHIL (exasperated). Kvetch, *kvetch*! Where are you from,
Mars?

MICHAEL. No. Pleasant Acres.

PHIL. Pleasant what? I thought you said you were from Ohio.

MICHAEL. Pleasant Acres is the name of the development we
live in.

PHIL. It sounds like a cemetery.

MICHAEL. I've often thought that's why we live there. See,
my family made its money operating a funeral home chain.

PHIL. Ooooh, gross!

MICHAEL. Relax. We never brought the customers home with
us.

PHIL. If nothing else, I guess it's steady work.

MARSHALL (knocking on the apartment door, offstage).
Michael? Michael, is Phil in there?

PHIL (calling toward the door). Yeah, Marsh. I'm in here.

MARSHALL (offstage). Are you decent?

PHIL (toward the door). What did you have in mind?

MICHAEL (toward the door). Come on in.

(MARSHALL, in characteristically odd attire, enters with a copy of the *Daily News*.)

PHIL. Join the party. You want some coffee?

MARSHALL. I don't have time. I've got a date in fifteen minutes.

PHIL. It's three-thirty in the morning!

MARSHALL. I get them when I can, okay? Listen, Della Vecchia, are you in a good mood?

PHIL. I've been in worse. Shoot.

MARSHALL. The Jones Beach management called your agency, and they called me while you were out. I don't know how to tell you this, but they've decided to close the show. You're supposed to pick up your severance pay in the morning. (He pulls out a candy bar and throws it at PHIL.) Here. I knew you'd need it. (PHIL throws the candy bar back at MARSHALL. To MICHAEL.) She even made the *Daily News* photo section. (He opens the paper.) It's the night owl edition. (To PHIL.) Where did you learn to swim?

PHIL. When it's a choice between that and sleeping with the fishes, you learn fast. (She grabs the paper.) Let me see that.

MARSHALL (looking over Phil's shoulder). Who are you trying to drown there?

PHIL. Morty. I wasn't drowning him. I was just teaching him a lesson.

MICHAEL. Luckily, the Coast Guard pulled her off his back before it was too late.

MARSHALL. Tough break about the show, Phil. What are you going to do now?

PHIL (standing). Now? Now I'm going home to my apartment, where I will fill the bathtub with lots of nice hot water. Then I will snuggle down into it and open my veins.

MARSHALL. Now there's the Philomena Della Vecchia I know and love.

PHIL. Goodnight, Michael. I'll see you tomorrow.

MICHAEL. Let me know if anything turns up.

PHIL. You want to make rounds together, Marshall?

MARSHALL (shaking his head). I don't think so. I'm safe for the next few weeks. That deodorant commercial I shot in April is still giving me residuals.

PHIL. Deodorant commercial? (This is too much of an effort and she shrugs.) I'm so tired, I'm gonna let that one pass. (She exits.)

MARSHALL. She must *really* be exhausted. Was it as bad as the paper made it sound?

MICHAEL (considering). Well, it wasn't the Titanic, but it ranked up there with the Andrea Doria.

MARSHALL. Sorry I missed it. What about the rest of the evening? Get anywhere with Phil?

MICHAEL. No!

MARSHALL. I'm not surprised. Few do. (He smirks and checks his watch.) Well, I'd better get downstairs. My date must be getting anxious. See you tomorrow.

MICHAEL. Night. (MARSHALL exits.)

(MIKE saunters in from the bedroom.)

MICHAEL (to himself). I'll just bet she's interested in me!

MIKE. Forget it, chump. She's not your type.

MICHAEL (turning to MIKE). How do you know? You weren't there tonight. This is one terrific girl. She's smart, she's pretty, she knows about all kinds of things.

MIKE. Like I said, not your type.

MICHAEL. Why not? What am I, a leper?

MIKE. No, just an Eagle Scout from Dayton. Come off it, Caldwell. You're just not in her league.

MICHAEL. Thank you very much. I can be exciting when I want to be!

MIKE. Yeah, you're a *million* laughs.

MICHAEL (in disgust). I'm going to bed. (He slams into the bathroom.)

MIKE (calling after MICHAEL). Don't forget to floss! (A pause.) I hope you don't take this too far. I think Phil is great, but *you* need someone a little more low-key. And besides, you came here to write, not date.

MICHAEL (from the bathroom, offstage). I just met her today!

MIKE (toward the bathroom). Maybe so, but I've seen the signs before. You act like a stuffed animal in heat. Will you please face facts for once? Phil's career comes first for her right now. You heard what she said about the Eric guy. For crying out loud, the woman lost her job tonight. The last thing she needs is you on her back. So stop fantasizing that anything is going to happen! Do you hear me?

("Space" music crashes through the apartment as the bathroom door flies open. MICHAEL, dressed a la Han Solo, with a ray gun in his right hand, rushes in. The bedroom door opens and PHIL, in full Princess Leia drag, swirls into the room. She meets MICHAEL at C. MICHAEL sweeps PHIL into his arms and whirls her in a circle, then carries her off to the bedroom and shuts the door. MIKE stands shaking his head as the lights go down.)

(Two months have passed. As the lights come up, MICHAEL

sits at his desk, working on a story. He writes, stares at it, crumples the paper, throws it on the floor, and repeats the process. After a minute of this, PHIL enters. Dressed to the hilt in "interview" clothes, she carries two "Bloomingdale's" shopping bags to C and drops them on the floor.)

PHIL. Why aren't I blond and stacked? Answer me that. (She reaches into the nearest bag and takes out a five-pound chocolate kiss, already half-eaten.) Because if I was blond and stacked, I could have gotten a job today. They were looking for a new swing girl for *Sugar Babies*. (She gnaws at the chocolate.)

MICHAEL. If you keep up these daily binges in Bloomingdale's deli section, the fact that you're dark and flat-chested won't be your only problem. You'll need a live-in dermatologist.

PHIL. Thank *you*, Doctor Kildare. I can't help this. Over the years, my depresssions and chocolate have established a special relationship. To break them up now would be cruel.

MICHAEL. I take it the Willy Wonka routine means that you didn't have any luck today.

PHIL. Define luck. I've had three immoral offers from agents and one chance to play a dancing zucchini in a *Seven Seas* commercial. Oh, yeah. A bag lady crossed Fifty-Third Street just to spit on me. Ask me again if I've had any luck today.

MICHAEL. How come you didn't take the commercial?

PHIL. What — and listen to Marshall whine all over my apartment? That kind of thing is *his* turf. This day should win some kind of an award for rotten.

MICHAEL. Oh, come on. It couldn't have been that bad.

TANYA (from outside the door, offstage). Yoo-hoos! Anyone being home?

PHIL (looking skyward). Thank you, God. My day is complete. The Anna Pavlova of the Upper East Side.

MICHAEL (calling toward the door). Yo, Tanya. Come on in.

(TANYA enters and closes the door behind her.)

TANYA. Misha, Tanya listens to fingers dancing across tippy-writer machine. Decide to come wisit. (To PHIL.) Hello to you, Phil. (She picks up the candy.) Still not working, and again with the big candy? Soon you will be looking like large football player, yes?

PHIL. That's right. (She grabs the candy from TANYA.) So shove off!

TANYA. Little Philomenka! Always with the jokes on Tanya! Is lucky Tanya knows you, kid, or she must be breaking your face. (To MICHAEL.) Misha, are you free to experience Tanya tonight?

MICHAEL. Could you clarify that one a little?

TANYA. Tanya dance tonight in new production of *Porgy and Bess*.

PHIL. I know I'm going to regret asking this. Who are *you* playing?

TANYA. Bess, naturally.

PHIL. Hasn't anyone mentioned that Bess is black, twinkletoes?

TANYA. Purely technicality. Tanya is *essence* of Bess. You see, Tanya has worked on collectivist farm in Soviet Union with many strapping young men. She understands the life of this woman — her struggles, her lusts. Especially her lusts.

PHIL. Come off it. There aren't any cotton farms in Russia!

TANYA. There are also no black people. My art overpowers these petty things.

PHIL. I'll bet. (There is a knock at the door.)

MICHAEL (toward the door). Who is it?

MARSHALL (calling from outside the door, offstage). Me. Close your eyes.

PHIL. What?

MARSHALL (from outside the door, offstage). That means you, too, Phil. I'm not coming in until everyone's eyes are closed.

TANYA. Oooh, Tanya love games!

MICHAEL (toward the door as ALL close their eyes). All right, our eyes are closed. Now what?

(MARSHALL tiptoes in, dressed for the first time in a civilized manner.)

MARSHALL. Open 'em.

MICHAEL (shocked). Will you look at this?

PHIL. Geez, Marsh. I don't get it. What are you supposed to be this time — the Preppy Poster Child?

MARSHALL (wounded). Thanks a lot. I thought it would be a nice change of pace to dress like other people.

PHIL (rising and circling MARSHALL). No, no, no, no. That would be too normal. There must be another reason for this. I'll get it in a minute. Don't tell me. Ah! Of course! You're out of work, aren't you? Join the crowd.

MARSHALL. Well, not really *out* of work. Tomorrow I'm doing a bit in the new Woody Allen movie shooting over in the park. Not much money — you know Woody — but it's a great little bit of business that is crucial to the ideas he's trying to express about modern society. Friday my agent has a meeting with Joe Papp's people to discuss some kind of Shakespeare-in-the-Park thing. Monday I've got a meeting with Fosse's staff about . . . (PHIL hands him the chocolate.) . . . nothing. Why didn't you stop me two lies ago?

PHIL. You were on a roll. I guess that leaves Tanya the only working person in the room.

MICHAEL (clearing his throat). Uh, Phil?

PHIL. Yeah, what is it?

MICHAEL. I didn't want to tell you before because I thought it might seem like bragging, but I'm working.

PHIL. Of course you are. And I'm sure that if you ever finish anything, it will be just peachy. But I'm talking paychecks at the moment.

MICHAEL (burned up). So am I. I sold a story yesterday.

PHIL. You're kidding! To whom?

MICHAEL. A magazine. Not a big one. I doubt if you've ever heard of it.

PHIL. Which one, for heaven's sake?

MICHAEL (mumbling). *Saturday Review*.

PHIL. Michael, cut it out!

TANYA. What you say?

MICHAEL (roaring). *Saturday Review*! (A moment, as the OTHERS digest this. PHIL sinks onto the couch.)

PHIL. You . . . *you* . . . sold a story to *Saturday Review*?

MICHAEL. Well, uh, yeah . . . yeah, I guess I sort of did.

PHIL (to MARSHALL). I'm gonna join the convent. What am I saying? *He* sold a story to *Saturday Review*. There *is* no God!

TANYA. Congratulations to you, Misha Caldwell. What is being wrong with you, Philomenka! Tanya is proud of her Misha. And she is not afraid to show this emotion. (She exits dramatically.)

MARSHALL (pointing to the door as he counts). Five, four, three, two, one. (There is an earsplitting scream from the hall.) Blastoff!

PHIL. Hey, how come you didn't mention this before? This is great! (MARSHALL gives her a look.) Really. When will the story be out?

MICHAEL. I don't know for sure. Next month, I think.

MARSHALL. What's the story about, Michael? Is it fiction?

MICHAEL (carefully). You might say that. It's about stuff.

New York stuff.

PHIL. That's precise. We can take a hint. If you want the story to be a surprise, just tell us.

MICHAEL. I want the story to be a surprise.

PHIL (angrily). What do you mean you want the story to be a surprise! We're your closest friends!

MARSHALL. Oh, leave him alone, Della Vecchia. We'll see it soon enough. Listen, you guys, anybody want to go Chinese?

PHIL (morosely). For starters.

MICHAEL (to MARSHALL). She's depressed.

PHIL. No, I *was* depressed. Now I'm suicidal. Your little success has pushed me into comatose. I may have to have intraveneous egg drop.

MARSHALL. That's the spirit, Phil. Okay, everybody grab some bucks and meet me in the lobby in ten minutes. (He exits.)

(MARHSALL pops his head back inside the door.)

MARSHALL. You want I should invite Tanya?

PHIL and MICHAEL. No!

MARSHALL. Just thought I'd ask. (He exits and closes the door behind him.)

PHIL. Why don't we take in a movie after dinner?

MICHAEL. We did that last night.

PHIL. So? Is there some kind of law against enjoying yourself two nights in a row?

MICHAEL. Enjoying yourself? Where's the entertainment in watching a bunch of high school kids get hacked to death on prom night? All that blood . . . and the two of you howling like lunatics. It was disgusting!

PHIL. Lighten up, Caldwell. Where's your sense of humor? Oh, I forget. You *like* proms. And speaking of comedy, any word from Cindy?

MICHAEL (thrown for a moment). No. I mean, yeah.

PHIL. I'll bite. What does *that* mean?

MICHAEL (lying). I got a letter from her yesterday, as a matter of fact.

PHIL. Sealed with a kiss, no doubt. What's new in Missouri?

MICHAEL. Ohio. And you know it.

PHIL. Don't be so touchy. From the Hudson west, who cares?

MICHAEL. Knock it off, Phil.

PHIL. So what did she have to say for herself? Does Barbie miss her Ken?

MICHAEL. Now that you mention it — yes!

PHIL. That's what I like. A woman with pride. Are you telling me she actually forgave you for leaving her flat?

MICHAEL. Yes, she did.

PHIL. So? You gonna leave on that midnight train to Dayton?

MICHAEL. I haven't had a chance to answer her yet.

PHIL (nastily). Come on! You've succeeded! You sold a story to *Saturday Review*! Now you can go back to Ohio, your thin little chest covered with merit badges, and spend the rest of your life as a potato head!

MICHAEL. Why do I have a sudden eerie feeling that you're not in a good mood?

PHIL. I am in a wonderful mood. I just feel a little indigestion coming on.

MICHAEL. What did you eat for lunch?

PHIL. Three helpings of Moo Goo Gai Pan and half an anchovy pizza.

MICHAEL. Sounds like toxic food shock.

PHIL. You got any Pepto?

MICHAEL (going to the refrigerator). Yeah, wait a minute.

PHIL. What kind of person keeps Pepto Bismol in the refrigerator?

MICHAEL. It's an old Ohio custom. (He hands PHIL the bottle.) Here, drink.

PHIL (after drinking). You know, in spite of yourself, you're really not that bad a guy, Caldwell.

MICHAEL. Gosh, thanks a *lot*.

PHIL. No, really. I mean it. You put up with me, don't you?

MICHAEL. That's not so hard.

PHIL. And you keep Pepto in the house. Let's face it. There aren't that many left like that. Most people just pop Tums. (A pause.) I don't think you have a malicious bone in your body.

MICHAEL (squirming, remembering the article). Oh, sure I do. Never mind all this. What movie do you want to see?

PHIL. I don't care. Let Marshall pick it. (A pause.) I'm sorry about just now. You're not mad, are you?

MICHAEL. No, of course not.

PHIL. Alright, I'll see you downstairs. And do me a favor and bring the Pepto, will you? (She exits.)

(MIKE strolls out of the bedroom.)

MIKE. What are you going to tell them when the story *does* come out? That it's only coincidental . . . the setting is an apartment house full of lunatics?

MICHAEL (hunting around the room for his money). Those people aren't lunatics.

MIKE. Michael, trust me. This place could be the uptown branch of Bellevue.

MICHAEL. Don't you think you're being a little hard on them? They're not going to take it personally. These people are sane, balanced adults.

TANYA (singing, offstage). I am lovink you, Porgies!

MICHAEL. See what I mean?

MIKE. There's ten dollars in your khaki pants. (MICHAEL exits to the bedroom.) Get serious! We are facing one of the greatest disasters of our time when that article hits the stands. Orson Welles may have to narrate!

MICHAEL (from the bedroom, offstage). Look, you're making me late. Put an egg in your shoe and beat it.

MIKE. Tres funny. Write your own stuff?

(MICHAEL appears at the bedroom door.)

MICHAEL. Everything will be fine, okay? I'm sure my harmless little satire isn't going to make waves. (He exits back into the bedroom.)

MIKE (to the audience). What you just heard were the famous last words of a *really* nice guy. (The lights go out.)

(It is a week later. As the lights come up, MICHAEL, PHIL and MARSHALL are grouped around a coffee table playing Scrabble. MICHAEL and PHIL are on the couch. MARSHALL sits on the floor, studying the board.)

MICHAEL (to PHIL). Your move. And try not to make it pornographic for a change.

PHIL (with a look at MICHAEL, putting down her tiles). Couth. C—o—u—t—h.

MARSHALL. How many points is that?

MICHAEL. Couth? What kind of a word is couth?

PHIL. You know, like the opposite of uncouth.

MICHAEL (smugly). It's not a word. The opposite of uncouth is cultured.

PHIL. Says who? When something's not clear, it's unclear. When something's not real, it's unreal. So if you're couth, you're not *un*-couth!

MARSHALL. My turn!

PHIL. Don't touch that tile!

MICHAEL.   Phil, take your tiles off and make a real word.

PHIL. Couth is a word! It had to be a word before they could put "un" in front of it! (To MARSHALL.) Doesn't "un" mean "not?"

MARSHALL (shrugging).   That's what the Seven-Up people tell me.

PHIL. There, you see?

MICHAEL. I don't want to fight about this. I'll just get the dictionary. (He gets up and goes to get the dictionary.)

PHIL. Don't you ever take a vacation from being a twerp? Were you the kid in high school with the protractor in his shirt pocket and all the extra looseleaf? (MARSHALL laughs. PHIL reads what MARSHALL has been putting down.) "Game drag. Us go eat." Always with the food!

MARSHALL. I didn't eat today! I had a wardrobe fitting for a new commercial.

PHIL. What are you shilling for this time?

MARSHALL. Malt liquor. And believe me, for what they're paying, Della Vecchia, it ain't shilling.

MICHAEL (looking through the dictionary but not showing anyone else). See? No such word. (PHIL goes to MICHAEL and tries to look at the dictionary. He slams it shut. He knows he is wrong but won't admit it.) I was right. (PHIL gives him a suspicious look.)

PHIL. You and Noah Webster must be very happy. Are you proud of yourself, humiliating me in front of one of our closest friends? (MARSHALL looks at her as if to say, "Who came in?") Oh, forget it! Look, it's four o'clock. According to my source, Richard Burton will be outside the Plaza Hotel at nine. Yes or no?

MICHAEL.   You mean you actually want to do that stupid groupie number again? I can't believe it! (To MARSHALL.)

We trailed Greta Garbo for ten blocks yesterday and she wouldn't even let me say "hello."

PHIL. Sometimes you're such a cetriuolo! *(Italian word, literally translated "cucumber." Used in Italy as insult equivalent to "jerk.")* You don't bother *her*! There are rules, Michael!

MARSHALL. Yeah. It would be uncouth. I've got plans for later on tonight anyway. I'm taking a chick to the Marx Brothers Festival at the Ziegfield. Sorry, Phil.

PHIL. Who'd you pay to go out with you this time, boy wonder?

MARSHALL (making a face at PHIL). I met her at the audition. She plays a waitress at the cantina.

MICHAEL. A waitress at the what?

MARSHALL. It would take too long to explain. Oh, that's what I wanted to talk to you about, Michael. I can set you up with one of my leftovers. Interested?

MICHAEL. It depends.

PHIL. On what? Is she humanoid? Don't trust him, Michael. Some of his leftovers violate the leash laws.

MARSHALL. Shut up, Phil. (To MICHAEL.) I've got an airline stewardess, a model, and the owner of the health food place around the corner.

PHIL. Nix.

MICHAEL. I can answer for myself, Phil. What are their names?

MARSHALL. Angelica, Heather, and Rainbow Skycloud.

PHIL. She sounds like a weather report. Wait a minute! I know her! She's that sixties throwback who never wears shoes. Scratch her, Caldwell, you have a karma deficiency.

MICHAEL (with a look at PHIL, trying to make her jealous). Any blondes?

MARSHALL. Heather is, sort of. You know models.

MICHAEL. She sounds cute.

PHIL. Just like a button. A tall, anorexic button. I take it this means I will be alone with Burton tonight? Well, it makes me no nevermind.

MARSHALL (producing a slip of paper). Here's her number. I told her you'd be calling.

MICHAEL. Isn't it short notice for a date?

MARSHALL. Not for Heather. Party is her middle name.

MICHAEL. How'd you know I'd pick her, anyway?

MARSHALL. I didn't. I told all three of them you'd be calling. (He checks his watch.) No time for food. I have to pick up the costumes before the store closes. See you later, Phil. And good luck with Heather, Michael. You'll need it. (He exits.)

MICHAEL. Costumes . . . I don't get it.

PHIL. Maybe you will tonight, if you wish real hard. (MICHAEL looks confused.) Aren't you going to call her?

MICHAEL. Sure. Why not? (He goes to the phone.) It'll be nice to get out for a change. (He reads the slip of paper and dials.) P—L—six—nine—three—one—one. Beat it, Phil.

PHIL. No way, Jose! I might learn something.

MICHAEL. Will you get out of here? I'll talk to you la . . . oh, hello. (PHIL tries to listen in on the conversation. She and MICHAEL circle each other as he talks into the phone.) Is this Heather? Oh, gee, I'm sorry, sir. Could I speak with her, please? (He covers the mouthpiece. To PHIL.) It was her roommate, Mr. Juan.

PHIL. I wonder if he's the same Mr. Juan who cuts my hair?

MICHAEL (into the phone). Hello, Heather? This is Michael Caldwell, a friend of Marshall Ryan's. . . . That's right. He mentioned that you might be interested in going out. I was wondering if you were free tonight, by any chance? . . . You are?

PHIL. *What* a coincidence!

MICHAEL (giving PHIL a dirty look, then back into the phone). What? . . . Oh, nothing. That was *my* roommate, Mr. Phil.

Anyway, Heather, I was thinking dinner. (He covers the mouthpiece, then speaks to PHIL.) Where can I take her that's nice?

PHIL (glibly). The Four Seasons.

MICHAEL (into the phone). I thought The Four Seasons would be nice. About eight o'clock? . . . Great. Where should I pick you up? (He writes something down.) Got it. See you then. 'Bye-'bye. (He hangs up and gloats.) How do you like them apples? It looks like Michael Stoddard Caldwell has a date with a fashion model.

PHIL (a pure shark). Wear your stilts. If Heather is the one I'm thinking of, she's nine feet tall and weighs forty-seven pounds. It'll be like dating the Matterhorn. You'd better call the restaurant and make reservations.

MICHAEL. Reservations?

PHIL. Yeah. It's one of those funny New York habits that probably hasn't made it to Dayton yet.

MICHAEL. How should I dress?

PHIL. Nothing spectacular. Just wear your moneybelt.

MICHAEL. Hold on a second here! How fancy *is* this place?

PHIL. I figure, for the two of you, a halfway decent meal will run you in the neighborhood of, say, two hundred and fifty bucks.

MICHAEL. *What*?

PHIL. That's wine included, of course. It's the most expensive place in town.

MICHAEL. Are you insane? I don't have that kind of money! What on earth made you suggest that place?

PHIL (innocently). I thought you wanted to show her a good time. Don't worry. I'm sure that fertile brain will come up with something. Arrivederci, Michael. (She exits. The lights go out.)

ACT TWO

SCENE: Michael's apartment, five hours later. The lights come up on MARSHALL, dressed in a Groucho Marx outfit. He is alone in the apartment and decidedly ill at ease.

MARSHALL (opening the door and calling out into the hall). Phil, get the lead out and haul it in here!

(PHIL enters the apartment with a bag.)

PHIL (surveying MARSHALL). May I say yet again that you look ridiculous?

MARSHALL. Lay off, will you? I'm passing up on a terrific date to do this. Not to mention the rental on this outfit!

PHIL. Rental? You shelled out bucks for that drag?

MARSHALL. Twenty-five bucks, to be exact. Plus another fifteen for the Harpo outfit my date was going to wear.

PHIL. It won't go to waste.

MARSHALL. I don't like this.

PHIL. Listen, you owe me one. I went out with your cousin Harold from Syracuse, didn't I?

MARSHALL. Harold's a nice guy.

PHIL. Are you going to force the truth out of me? My image of Mr. Right does not feature a man with pink hair and a safety pin through his ear!

MARSHALL. Is it my fault punk rock just hit Syracuse?

PHIL. Drop it, okay? Help me with these things.

MARSHALL (as PHIL pulls some glasses from the bag). Oh, Phil. Not the dribble glasses! This is low!

PHIL. It always works.

MARSHALL. Yeah, but still . . .

PHIL. Are you going to help me or not? (She fumbles through the bag.)

MARSHALL. What are you looking for now? (PHIL pulls a sexy nightgown from the bag.) Oh, no! I don't want to be involved in this. No way! (He starts for the door.)

PHIL. Get back here!

MARSHALL. This is too much.

PHIL (as MARSHALL continues to exit). Marshall, did I tell you that a really good friend of mine from Equity is marrying a director who's doing a play at Circle in the Square?

MARSHALL (as he opens the door to leave). So? (He exits, closing the door behind him.)

PHIL (opening the door and speaking into the hallway). So, he can't start rehearsals because he can't find a good enough unknown for the male lead. He asked me if I knew anyone who'd fit the bill.

(After a moment, MARSHALL pops his head back in.)

PHIL (matter-of-factly). He trusts my intuition.

MARSHALL. Did you mention anyone we know?

PHIL. Not yet. But I could. (MARSHALL walks back into the room and PHIL throws the nightgown at him.) You disgust me, you know that? Now put that in an obvious place.

MARSHALL (placing the nightgown over the chair back). Why are you going to all this trouble anyway?

PHIL. Do you want Michael to get stuck with some dizzy blonde for the rest of his life?

MARSHALL. It's just one lousy date! Besides, what makes you think she'll want *him*?

PHIL. Senility setting in already? I've met Heather. Michael meets all her requirements. He's male and he's breathing.

MARSHALL. I still think you're making too much of this. The girl is a model! She can pick and choose.

PHIL. I can't afford to take any chances.

MARSHALL. *You* can't afford to take any chances? What difference does Michael having a date make to you? (The lights begins to dawn.) Unless . . . do you . . . oh, no . . . you . . . and *him*? I don't believe it!

PHIL. What don't you believe?

MARSHALL. I just never thought of the two of you as . . . why don't you just tell him how you feel instead of going through all this?

PHIL. And set myself up for rejection? Forget it!

MARSHALL. Why would he reject you? You're a great girl! You're attractive, you're talented, you're sensitive, sort of. You don't have to stoop to this.

PHIL. Are you on drugs?

MARSHALL. What?

PHIL. Who is this person who just said these things to me? And where has he been hiding for the past two years?

MARSHALL. So I had a temporary lapse into humanity. What are you going to do, take away my birthday?

PHIL. I'm just surprised, that's all.

MARSHALL. What is this — everyone but Marshall has feelings? If I'm cut, do I not bleed?

PHIL (going for MARSHALL). Let's find out!

MARSHALL. Take off, Della Vecchia! You know, I'm getting pretty sick and tired of being considered the man of stone around here. I don't need the abuse.

PHIL. So you think I should take the adult approach? Go to him and lay it on the line? "This is how it is and what do you intend to do about it?"

MARSHALL. You could be a little more subtle. I know. Try it out on me.

PHIL. Get out of here!

MARSHALL. No, really. Come on. I'll be Michael.

PHIL (reluctantly). Okay. (She squares off with MARSHALL, then clears her throat.) Michael?

MARSHALL (brightly). Yeah?

PHIL. You know, we've known each other for a couple of months now and I think something's beginning to happen.

MARSHALL. Too vague.

PHIL. You think so?

MARSHALL. Definitely. You need a stronger beginning.

PHIL. How about if I just tear his shirt off?

MARSHALL. Start over!

PHIL. Michael, I think you should know that I'm feeling . . . something inside that's –

MARSHALL (interrupting). Nope. Now you sound like a Hallmark card. What's the matter with you? You've never been at a loss for words before! Do it again!

PHIL. Okay! (Each time she starts, her voice changes and MARSHALL shakes his head "no.") Michael, have you noticed . . . Michael, I've been finding myself . . . Michael . . . Michael . . . (She and MARSHALL look at each other in frustration.)

MARSHALL. What else do you have in the bag?

PHIL. A Don Ho record collection.

MARSHALL. What?

PHIL (taking the records out of the bag and looking through them). *A Don Ho Christmas* . . . you should hear the *Ave*

Maria played on a ukelele . . . *Don Ho in Tahoe, Don Ho's Hawaii,* and, of course, the ever-popular *Don Ho: Live at Philharmonic Hall.*

MARSHALL. Pretty good. But what's the point? Caldwell doesn't have a stereo.

PHIL (arranging the records and standing back to gauge the effect). All the better! She'll think he bought them for the album covers! (The lights go out.)

(It is nine o'clock that same night. The lights come up and, after a moment, MICHAEL and HEATHER enter the apartment. HEATHER is stunning which is nice because when she opens her mouth, she reveals the intelligence of a small electric appliance light fixture. MICHAEL carries a bag filled with take-out Japanese food.)

HEATHER (whining). I think we should have stayed. The Maitre'd said the table would be ready in fifteen minutes. We could have sat at the bar and had cocktails and everything.

MICHAEL (with false heartiness). A place like that has no business making its clientele wait for a table they reserved. I expected more out of them.

HEATHER. But take-out Japanese! I got all dressed up for this date.

MICHAEL. And you look very pretty. (He starts to set out the food packages.)

HEATHER. Well, I should hope so! Juan spent all afternoon contouring my cheekbones!

MICHAEL. Please, sit down and make yourself comfortable.

HEATHER (looking at MICHAEL blankly). Are you kidding? Do you know how long it took me to get into this outfit without wrinkling it? Women do not dress like this to be comfortable! Why did you think I stood in the subway train on the way over?

MICHAEL. I was wondering about that. Your feet must be killing you.

HEATHER. I'm a model, silly. I'm used to my feet killing me. Like they say, it comes with the territory.

MICHAEL. But you would have sat down if we'd stayed at The Four Seasons.

HEATHER. Not necessarily.

MICHAEL. How do you eat?

HEATHER. Who would have *eaten*? At a place like that you just mingle. There are always so many interesting people to talk to and *everything*. I was really looking forward to tonight. I told a lot of people I'd *be* there! (She sighs.) Oh, well. Their loss, right?

MICHAEL. Uh, right.

HEATHER. So? (She strikes a modeling pose.) What do you think?

MICHAEL. About what?

HEATHER. About the outfit! Since you're the only one who's going to see it. I wore it in last month's issue of *Harper's Bazaar*. Don't you just love these French sleeves? They are pure genius. Really *in* now, too. Part of the pirate look. That session was great. In one shot, this guy dressed like Bluebeard posed with me. It was wild. He wore a kerchief with a skull on it and little bones and *everything*!

MICHAEL. Modeling must be . . . uh . . . fun.

HEATHER. Oh, it *is*. But do not be misled. I mean, it does take a *lot* of dedication. Photography is a very high art form, you know. Really! And so much of it depends on me. I mean, I have a lot of *real* responsibility. If I'm not beautiful, well, everything is just ruined. Luckily that's never been a problem.

MICHAEL. Won't you sit down and have some sushi? I think

it's starting to get cold.

HEATHER. It's supposed to be cold, silly! Haven't you ever had Japanese food before?

MICHAEL. Not really.

HEATHER. Oh, it's terrific stuff. It's got protein and vittamins and *everything*!

MICHAEL. Vittamins?

HEATHER. Vitamins, silly! (Disgusted, she sits.) I may as well sit down. That's just the way Vidal Sassoon says it. Sometimes I think he says it that way just for effect, but isn't it a rush? I just love men with English accents! I mean, I really do! Like once, I went to London to do this raincoat layout. Anyway, everybody talked with these accents. It was like living with the *Beatles* or something! The only thing is that they're kinda uppity about it, you know? Like I remember telling my bellhop outside the lift — that means elevator in English — anyway, I said, "Hey, you know, I just *love* your accent!" and he said, "I don't have an accent, *you* do." I don't know what he meant by *that*! See what I mean about uppity? But I got over it. I think a man with an English accent could tell me to jump off a cliff or something and I'd just *do* it, I mean, I really would! I'm such a sucker! (She laughs.) Don't you think that's funny?

MICHAEL. Uh, sure.

HEATHER (studying MICHAEL). I wish you had one.

MICHAEL. What?

HEATHER. An English accent! Haven't you been listening to me?

MICHAEL. I'm sorry. Sounds like you've modeled in some interesting places.

HEATHER. You bet. Like once, I got to go to Barcelona. It was on the way to Rome where I shot a lingerie spread in St. Peter's Square. Was *that* ever an experience! Don't those

Swiss Guards ever see women? I mean, foam at the mouth, and in front of the Pope and *everything*! (She catches herself.) Oh, you're not Catholic, are you?

MICHAEL. No, I'm Methodist.

HEATHER. Really? I was raised a Mormon, but have since embraced Buddhism. See, I went to a party at this photographer's apartment? Anyway, we wound up chanting all night. Did me in forever and *then* some. Everything just became so clear! Do you think my eyes are too far apart? I was once heavily involved with this guy who broke up with me because he said my eyes were too far apart. How superficial can you get! I know they're not! Any sushi left? (MICHAEL hands her some food.) Thanks. Thinking back, I really gave him too much credit. I mean, I thought he was deeper than that. But I guess I have to learn that not everyone is going to have the depth that I have. And I know that bothers people.

MICHAEL. What does?

HEATHER. The fact that I'm different from them. Average people get really jealous of that. Oh, well. At least I have Juan. He understands. He just accepts me for the eccentric that I am.

MICHAEL. Why would anyone give you a hard time? I wouldn't say you're eccentric.

HEATHER (standing). I am so eccentric! Everybody says I am!

MICHAEL. Sorry!

HEATHER. I looked it up! Eccentric means different and I'm a lot better looking than most people. And I'm hated for it! (She becomes calmer.) But I'll survive. You know that song, *I Will Survive*? I'm telling you, someone knows what's going on in my life, because that song is my *motto*! Really. Do you have a weight problem?

MICHAEL (confused). Uh, no.

HEATHER (matter-of-factly). Me, either. (She sits down on the couch and crosses her legs. After a pause, she looks around the room in boredom, then sighs. MICHAEL becomes uncomfortable and tries to start up a conversation again.)

MICHAEL. So, you're a friend of Marshall's?

HEATHER. Yeah. I mean, I know him. I guess we're friends. You know how it is, though. You can never be sure about some people. Like whether or not you're really friends? Some people always have a motive behind everything they do. Like they can act one way in front of you but then they're really thinking something entirely different deep down. Like even with Marshall. I mean, what was he thinking when he set us up together? Do you think he had some kind of motive behind it? It makes you wonder. I mean, what's in this for *him*? (MICHAEL looks a bit dejected.) Hey, don't take it personally or anything. I mean, life itself is just one big question mark, you know? But my aim is to take that question mark and make it into one giant exclamation point where everything is a new and exciting trip. I think that's why I love to act. It gives me the chance to experience other people's lives.

MICHAEL. I didn't know you were an actress.

HEATHER. Marshall didn't tell you that we met at an acting class? Oh, well. Yes, I am.

MICHAEL. What do you plan to pursue?

HEATHER (huffing). Acting, silly!

MICHAEL. No, I mean a theatrical career, films?

HEATHER. Oh. (She pauses.) Well, I don't really care. I just want to participate in something that will touch people. But just between you and me, my big dream is to get into soap.

MICHAEL. Soap? Like Palmolive?

HEATHER (huffing). No, soap like soap operas, silly! Soap operas are a very high art form, you know. They are so true to life! Don't you take any in?

MICHAEL. No.

HEATHER. Well, you should! The things I have learned! I mean, how to cope and everything! Those poor people! The problems they have to face! (She stops and looks pensively into space.) Makes you feel like you're not alone, you know? (A short pause.) You write, right?

MICHAEL. Right.

HEATHER. Well, I think that's great, you know why? Because I read all the time! Really! Drives Juan absolutely crazy! See, he spends most of his free time taking in high levels of sound. (MICHAEL is confused. She looks at MICHAEL and huffs again.) *Music*!

MICHAEL. What kind of stuff do you read?

HEATHER.   Harlequin, Candlelight Ecstasy, Silhouette Romance. All different kinds of things. Have you ever tried Indonesian food?

MICHAEL (startled). No. I've been meaning to for months but somehow there never seems to be enough time.

HEATHER. You should try it. It's the total food experience. I live on it.

MICHAEL. All the time?

HEATHER. When I'm not fasting. But not just any kind of Indonesian food. See, the best kind comes from this tribe in the outback.

MICHAEL (amazed). The what?

HEATHER. Outback! It's like a place they have behind their cities. Anyway, the tribe has opened up this place on Second Avenue. It's really vogue. And they use the best spices. The pepper alone causes self-purification. Last week, after dinner, I found myself sitting in the bathtub reliving my birth! Then I started to get real paranoid and I was crying and screaming for six hours! It was great! Finally, I had to get my stomach pumped. Hey, your eye just twitched! Am I making you tense? Are you feeling tense? Tension causes death, you know!

MICHAEL (obviously nervous). We're all going to die anyway. Why not help it along?

HEATHER. Now you're hostile. You've got to get rid of your hostility! Just tell yourself, "No way. No hostile vibes for me. Abu-gamma. Abu-gamma." Chant that for an hour. It works! Can I have some sake?

MICHAEL. Sure. (He gets the sake and looks around for some glasses.)

HEATHER. Where do you keep your sake glasses?

MICHAEL. My what?

HEATHER. Your sake glasses, silly! You're only supposed to drink sake from those cute little cups that look like eggshells cut in half!

MICHAEL. I don't have anything like that. (He spots the dribble glasses.) Will these do?

HEATHER (pouting). I guess they'll have to, but it would have been more authentic and everything if you had sake glasses. Everybody else I know has them.

MICHAEL. I told you before, I've never had Japanese food! Why would I have little eggshells for their booze?

HEATHER. See? You *are* tense!

MICHAEL. I'm not!

HEATHER. Then why are you biting my head off? This has not been an easy time for me. First, no Four Seasons. Then you take me to this hole and now, no sake glasses! Why are you doing this to me? I have to be on top of the Port Authority Building at six a.m. tomorrow morning looking beautiful! Do you have any idea how difficult that is? I need tranquility!

MICHAEL (desperately). Why don't you just try the sake? Maybe it'll help you relax a little, huh?

HEATHER. Forget it! I've lost that sake feeling! Wait till I tell Juan about this! No sake glasses and you've never had raw fish before!

MICHAEL (doing a take). What did you say?

HEATHER (in an exact tone of voice). "Forget it! I've lost that sake feel—"

MICHAEL (cutting HEATHER off). No, the part about the raw fish.

HEATHER. What did you think the sushi was, soybeans?

MICHAEL. Are you telling me I just ate raw fish?

HEATHER. What difference does it make?

MICHAEL (feeling sick). I think I feel a technicolor yawn coming on.

HEATHER. You want to go to the movies *now*?

MICHAEL. Not exactly. If you'll excuse me . . . (He runs for the bathroom and slams the door shut. HEATHER shrugs her shoulders and reaches for the sake. As she raises a glass to her lips, the dribble effect sloshes the liquid down the front of her blouse. She brushes it off angrily and moves to the chair with the nightgown, which she notices for the first time.)

(As HEATHER examines the nightgown, PHIL opens the apartment door and pops her head into the room. Dressed like Chico Marx, she looks around quickly for MICHAEL, then beckons TANYA, dressed like Harpo, and MARSHALL, dressed like Groucho, into the room after her.)

HEATHER. He's a psycho! (She turns to flee the room and is confronted by the OTHERS. She whirls around, presses her hands to her temples, and closes her eyes.) Abu-gamma! Abu-gamma!

MARSHALL (a la Groucho). Abu-gamma to you, too, lady.

PHIL (a la Chico). Whassamatta, you no feel-a too good? I got justa da ting. I scream, you scream, we alla scream for ice scream!

MARSHALL (a la Groucho). Leave her alone, you.

HEATHER. What are you doing?

MARSHALL (a la Groucho). I'm fighting for your honor, which is more than you ever did.

PHIL (a la Chico). Atsa good one, boss.

MARSHALL (a la Groucho, leaning his head on Heather's shoulder and yearning up at her). Can I have a lock of your hair?

HEATHER. No!

MARSHALL (a la Groucho). You're lucky. I was going to ask for the whole wig.

HEATHER. Oh, my God! You're *all* psychos!

MARSHALL (a la Groucho). I'd horsewhip you for that, if I had a horse. (TANYA creeps up on HEATHER and begins to maneuver her around the couch.)

PHIL (a la Chico). Don'ta be scared, lady. He's a-been house-broken!

HEATHER (to TANYA). You just stay away from me, that's all! Just stay away from me! (She runs out the front door. PHIL and MARSHALL follow her.)

(MICHAEL comes out of the bathroom.)

TANYA (calling after PHIL and MARSHALL). You are right, Phil. This *is* big-time fun! (She runs out after the OTHERS.)

MICHAEL (tentatively). Heather? (The lights go out.)

(It is six a.m., the following morning. The lights come up on MICHAEL, asleep on the couch. The debris of the night before litters the apartment. MICHAEL is fully dressed and has his hand under the pillow. After a moment, PHIL and MARSHALL, dressed in pajamas, tiptoe in.)

PHIL (looking around the apartment, in a stage whisper). Where *is* that thing? (She creeps around the room.) I know it's got to be here! It's the only place left. I retraced all my steps last night and nothing!

MARSHALL (in a stage whisper). How stupid can you get — losing your wallet?

PHIL. Try not to be *too* sympathetic!

MARSHALL. Well, you should have been more careful.

PHIL. Do you always have to pick times like *this* to start with the lectures?

MARSHALL. Sorry. It's just that I don't particularly want to face Caldwell this morning.

PHIL. Just shut up! Do you think this is *my* idea of fun? Now, keep looking! The sooner we find it, the sooner we can get out of here!

MARSHALL. Don't tell *me* to shut up! You shouldn't have pulled the whole number in the first place!

PHIL. Who helped, kemosabe?

MARSHALL. I didn't want to!

PHIL. Did I put a gun to your head? Now, look!

MARSHALL (after a fruitless ransacking of the apartment). Can't you afford a new wallet?

PHIL. I've had that one since high school. It has all my important stuff in it.

MARSHALL. What — your Bloomingdale's charge card?

PHIL. Among other things.

MARSHALL. Like what? Subway tokens?

PHIL. Try my laminated miniature copy of my diploma from the N.Y.C.H.S.P.A.

MARSHALL. The what?

PHIL. The New York City High School for the Performing Arts. Go ahead and laugh. All I had to do was flash it and I got into *Fame* for free. (She stands over the couch and stretches out her hands toward MICHAEL.) What did you do with that wallet? (Michael's hand comes out from under the pillow with the wallet.)

MARSHALL (in a normal voice). Let's hope he's sleepwalking. For heaven's sake, grab it and run!

MICHAEL. Not so fast.

MARSHALL. She made me do it, Michael. I swear. It was all her idea. I'll be running along now. See you later, Phil. (He exits quickly.)

PHIL (after MARSHALL). Count on it! (To MICHAEL.) So, uh, what's new? Had breakfast yet? Hungry? I'll whip you up some Wheaties. (MICHAEL just glares at her.) Not a morning person, are you? Or did you just get up on the wrong side of the couch? (A pause, as MICHAEL glares.) Into mime? Come on, Marcel Marceau, you've made your point. You're angry.

MICHAEL. I am not angry. I am furious.

PHIL. Oh, yeah? Why?

MICHAEL (evenly). Don't play dumb over this one, Philomena. Heather called me at four a.m. this morning and told me everything down to the last gory detail.

PHIL. I don't have any idea what you're talking about.

MICHAEL. Yes, you do. Your fine hand was behind the whole caper.

PHIL (giving in). Atsa right, boss. What gave it away?

MICHAEL. Since when does Harpo speak with a Russian accent? Since when does Harpo *speak*?

PHIL. I guess you got me on that one, boss.

MICHAEL. Heather only mentioned *three* Marx Brothers. No Zeppos available?

PHIL. Edna was at Tootie's.

MICHAEL (pacing around the room, tossing the wallet up and down). Now, I think you owe me an explanation.

PHIL. Can't I just have my wallet? Just give me the wallet. I'll leave and you can sit here and pout for the next forty-eight hours. Then we'll be friends again.

MICHAEL. Uh-uh.

PHIL. Well, what do you expect? Shall I throw myself at your mercy and beg for forgiveness?

MICHAEL. It wasn't a nice thing to do.

PHIL. Is fun against your religion? Abu-gamma! Abu-gamma! Okay! Okay! So I eavesdrop, too! Shoot me!

MICHAEL. Can't a person have a little privacy? Don't I deserve at least *that*? (A pause.) Now you've got me screaming!

PHIL. That's great!

MICHAEL. Why? Screaming doesn't help. It never solves anything.

PHIL. There you go again. Mister Control. You have a problem, you solve it. Not everything in life is that simple. (As HEATHER.) You know, life itself is really just one big question mark! (MICHAEL fights back laughter for a moment, then BOTH break up laughing and sit on the couch.)

MICHAEL. I guess I wasn't having such a great time. Heather was a little strange.

PHIL. Heather was a little strange the way the Atlantic Ocean is a little wet.

MICHAEL. Maybe so, but that doesn't excuse what you three did.

PHIL. If you're waiting for me to grovel, don't hold your breath, kiddo.

MICHAEL. It was childish, that's all!

PHIL. Are you really mad?

MICHAEL. Yes.

PHIL. Then I guess the night wasn't a total loss.

MICHAEL. And just what is that supposed to mean?

PHIL. It's the first human emotion you've shown in three

months.

MICHAEL. What?

PHIL. Never mind. I'm sorry. Really, I am. Forgive me?

MICHAEL. Do I have a choice?

PHIL. No. Take me to breakfast. I'm starved.

MICHAEL. You take me. There's seventeen dollars in your wallet.

PHIL (outraged). You looked in my wallet?

MICHAEL. Yeah. I've never seen that many charge cards. I was almost blinded by the relection off the plastic.

PHIL. Did you take anything?

MICHAEL. Nothing. Although I have to admit your membership card to the Monkees' fan club was pretty tempting.

PHIL. It'll be worth something someday.

MICHAEL. Is that the reason you kept the picture of Sonny Bono?

PHIL. He came with the wallet. And besides, when you're Italian, there are some loyalties you just can't explain. Is there anything else you want to ridicule in here?

MICHAEL. No, I think that covers it.

PHIL. Where do you want to eat?

MICHAEL. Zabar's.

PHIL. Zabar's? Just to breathe the cream cheese and lox in that place costs!

MICHAEL. Uh-huh.

PHIL. Oh, I get it. I always thought you were too big a person for revenge.

MICHAEL. Think again. I'm going to eat you out of next month's rent.

PHIL. I hope you choke on the smallest thing you swallow. Fifteen minutes?

MICHAEL. Thirty. I need to shower.

PHIL. Meet me at the elevator. (She starts to leave.)

MICHAEL. Phil?

PHIL. What is it?

MICHAEL. You forget Don.

PHIL. Right. (She gathers up the records and exits.)

(MRS. CALDWELL enters from the bedroom.)

MRS. CALDWELL. That is a very strange girl.

MICHAEL. Tell me about it.

MRS. CALDWELL. Are you ready to come home now?

MICHAEL. No! She's finally showing some interest.

MRS. CALDWELL. That's what worries me. You don't want a girl like that.

MICHAEL. Oh, yes, I do!

MRS. CALDWELL. But why? You had Cindy Evans in Dayton.

MICHAEL. Mother, I realize you have my best interests at heart, but I am not in love with Cindy Evans.

MRS. CALDWELL. Thank God! I hated her, anyway. But, honey — and I mean this with all my heart — I hate *that* one even more. She's so . . . so . . .

MICHAEL. Italian?

MRS. CALDWELL. That, too. Your coming here was a big mistake. A mother knows.

MICHAEL. Don't you want me to be happy?

MRS. CALDWELL. Not as much as I want *me* to be happy. Shall I help you pack?

(MIKE enters from the bedroom.)

MIKE. Keep your paws off the luggage, toots.

MRS. CALDWELL (recoiling). It's *him* again!

MIKE (to MICHAEL). Phil is the first woman you've known who was worth the effort.

MRS. CALDWELL. Why should he be the one who has to make all the effort?

MICHAEL. That's right! Why should I?

MIKE. It must have slipped your mind for a minute. You're in love with her. She's not yet in love with you.

MRS. CALDWELL. If she's not in love with you, then what's keeping you here? I don't think she'd care if you *did* come home.

MIKE. I think she'd care.

MICHAEL. Yeah, sure. She'd cry her eyes out for about thirty seconds.

MIKE. No, really. You're not seriously thinking of going back to Dayton, are you?

MICHAEL. No, of course not. But it would serve her right if I did.

(PHIL floats out of the bedroom, dressed a la Scarlett O'Hara, as sweeping music is heard.)

PHIL. Oh, Michael, Michael, it's nevuh been Ashley. It's you! It's you! Hold me and crush me in yoah arms!

MICHAEL (as Rhett Butler). No, Phil. You had my heart at your feet and you walked over it.

MIKE (burying his head in his hands). Oh, my God!

PHIL. But if you go back to Ohio, where will I go? What will I do?

MICHAEL. Frankly, my dear, I don't give a darn.

MIKE. Damn, you idiot!

MICHAEL. What?

MIKE. The line is damn, not darn! (PHIL flings herself onto the couch in a tableau of broken womanhood as the lights fade out.)

(It is three days later. As the lights come up, MICHAEL sits disconsolately at his typewriter. He watches MIKE read a copy of *Saturday Review* on the couch.)

MIKE. I can't believe you wrote this! And you'd better hope they can't either or they'll tear your arms off!

MICHAEL. Will you please shut up! I feel bad enough about the whole thing without having my nose rubbed in it.

MIKE (reading). I didn't know Phil had a nose job.

MICHAEL. How do you know I meant Phil? I didn't use real names. That character could be any one of a hundred people!

MIKE (witheringly). Oh, right. (He reads aloud.) "Among the other apartment dwellers was an unemployed actress named Concetta Contadina." Now, why on earth would Phil think you meant her? If I were you, Michael . . . and I am, come to think of it . . . I'd start packing.

MICHAEL. Don't be ridiculous. How mad can they get? (There is a piercing scream from Tanya's apartment.)

TANYA (from offstage). I kill you!

MIKE. Now, who could that be? Oh, yeah. (He reads.) "Nijinsky in drag." Right. How mad can they get?

TANYA (from offstage). Get me ax!

MIKE. Well, time to be going. I hate senseless violence, especially when there's good reason for it. Nighty-night, kid. (He exits. MICHAEL walks over to the couch and picks up the *Saturday Review*. He leafs through it until there is a knock on the door. He jumps and stashes the magazine under a pile of papers on his desk.)

(PHIL breezes in, obviously excited.)

PHIL. You're not going to believe this! I got a job!

MICHAEL. Phil, that's great! (There is the sound of breaking plaster from upstairs.)

PHIL. What was that? It sounded like Tanya just punched out her living room.

TANYA (from offstage). Aaaargh! I am coming for you, Misha Caldwell!

MICHAEL (nervously to PHIL). We're playing a game. Sort of a Russian Hide and Go Seek. Violence is a big part of it. Never mind that. What kind of job did you get?

PHIL. Sit down! (MICHAEL sits.) This is so thrilling, you're not going to believe it. I don't believe it myself! Yours truly, c'est moi, is going to play Katharine Hepburn's — yes, Mr. and Mrs. America and all the ships at sea — I said Katharine, we're not talking Audrey here — Katharine Hepburn's grand-daughter in a new play! How deluxe can you get! I even got to meet her! I'll remember it for the rest of my life!

MICHAEL. What did she say?

PHIL (straight out front, doing Hepburn). "Would you mind letting go of my hand? My arm is getting numb." We start rehearsals September seventeenth. (She sings.) "Give my regards to Broadway, remember me to Herald Square —"

MICHAEL (cutting PHIL off). You're really hyper! Do you want some chocolate?

PHIL. Are you out of your mind? I have to lose weight before rehearsals! Miss Katharine Hepburn will not want to appear onstage with the Goodyear Blimp, bucko! From now on, it's starvation city. (She sits next to MICHAEL.) I am so excited. This play could be my big break. You know, Christopher Reeve got his start in a play with her. Maybe I will, too. I can see it now. *Superman Six: The Sex Change.* (MICHAEL laughs.) But this is a chance for me. It's the first time I'll be able to show what I can do as a serious actor.

MICHAEL (hugging PHIL). I know how you feel. Every time I look out the window and realize I'm in New York writing, I get the same feeling. (Embarrassed by the sudden physical contact, PHIL and MICHAEL break apart.)

PHIL (covering). Oh, will you listen to me? I'm running on and on and here you are being so nice and I haven't even asked how your latest project's going!

MICHAEL. Okay, I guess. I'm ghosting a piece for *True Confessions* to pay the rent.

PHIL. Yeah? (She crosses to the typewriter.) I read that stuff when I was in the seventh grade. (She reads the title.) "I Sold My Baby for a Weedeater." Nobody's gonna buy that!

MICHAEL. Oh, no? Listen to last month's issue: "The Bride Wore Cleats." "The Babysitter Ate Our Dog." "My Husband Won Me in a Poker Game." Had enough?

PHIL. More than enough. (She spies the *Saturday Review*.) Michael! Why didn't you tell me that the issue was out? What page is it on?

MICHAEL (now that the fat is on the fire). Don't read it now! Let's go out and celebrate your job! We can go to Sardi's and see who comes in or something!

PHIL. Cool your jets. I'm trying to read.

MICHAEL. The Mr. Universe Contest is at the Garden!

PHIL. Who wants to watch a bunch of not so incredible hulks grease up?

MICHAEL. Do we have to waste the night cooped up here? (Now totally out of character.) This is New York! There's lots going on out there! The article isn't that great anyway. You know *Saturday Review* — all that highbrow junk. Let's go somewhere! (He is desperate.) Anywhere! These feet are itchin' to ramble, toots! (PHIL laughs.) What's so funny?

PHIL. The people in the story seem vaguely familiar. (She reads aloud.) "One of the tenants was in an artistic rut. He breathed life into inanimate objects. His specialty was cocktail vegetables." Marshall is going to die!

MICHAEL. Why do you bring him up?

PHIL. Oh, come *on*, Michael. "Cocktail vegetables." Real ace camouflage.

MICHAEL. You think he'll get angry?

PHIL. Why should he? If he gives you any grief, just tell him he was your inspiration. He'll buy it. Besides, Marshall isn't stupid. He'll know it's just a parody.

MICHAEL. I can't tell you how glad I am to hear you say that, Phil.

PHIL. Huh?

MICHAEL. You can finish it later. Let's *go* someplace!

PHIL. Michael, I know this couldn't possibly be the case, but is there some reason why you don't want me to read this?

MICHAEL. Yes.

PHIL. That's what I thought. (She reads further. MICHAEL is in agony. Phil's eyes widen in disbelief when she gets to the part about herself. She gives MICHAEL a look, then reads aloud.) "Among the other apartment dwellers was an un-employed actress named Concetta Contadina." (She slowly turns and looks at MICHAEL, who gives her a big, toothy, insincere smile.) "I liked her, but it was soon apparent that her feelings for me were a trifle stronger. She declared her undying passion over endless cups of espresso." (In shock, Phil's eyes scan the article and she reads on in mounting rage.) "Frequent-ly, I would find her waiting for me by the elevator. Her eyes smoldered with Latin fire. And there *I* was . . . just a gentle, quiet guy from the midwest, transformed virtually overnight into her Neopolitan love-god." (To MICHAEL.) *Love-god*? *You* were *my* love-god?

MICHAEL. You said yourself that it was a parody. So I padded it a little!

PHIL (totally enraged). How could you do this to me! All the time I thought we were friends! I open up to you, spill my guts, and you make like a Hoover upright in the name of creative talent!

MICHAEL. Phil, I . . .

PHIL. You know what should happen to you, you little troll? You should be killed. Slowly. Then you should be brought back to life and killed again!

MICHAEL. Can't we talk about this?

PHIL. Why? You need material for a sequel?

MARSHALL (from offstage). Michael? Michael? Are you in there?

MICHAEL. Marshall! Oh, my God! Uh, come on in.

(MARSHALL, dressed as a matador, enters the apartment.)

MARSHALL. Phil, great to see you.

PHIL. Hi, Marsh. Cute threads. Have you seen the latest issue of —

MICHAEL (interrupting PHIL). Sit down and make yourself comfortable, Marshall. Let me take your cape. How did the beer commercial go?

MARSHALL. It was just swell. In fact, we even finished early. You see, one of the guys on the crew was reading *this*. (He produces the *Saturday Review* from under his cape.) And he was laughing so hard we had to stop shooting. I want to congratulate you for destroying what little career I had!

PHIL. You mean it's on the newstands already? Quick, Marshall, how much money do you have?

MARSHALL. About thirty dollars.

PHIL. Not enough to buy up New York. I am ruined! At this very moment, Katharine Hepburn is reading that article. (MARSHALL does a take.) Any minute now, she is going to call William Morris and get me canned as a lunatic!

MARSHALL. What are *you* so mad about? I'm the one who's really suffering because of this! Thanks to him, I will probably lose the beer commercial. And the beet commercial. (He withers.) Not to mention all the other cocktail vegetables in my repertoire.

PHIL. Do you honestly think that dressing like a moron is a vital contribution to the arts?

MARSHALL. So what do *you* have lined up, Sophia Loren? The last play you were in is at the bottom of Zach's Bay!

(TANYA throws open the apartment door.)

TANYA. I have come for you, Misha Caldwell!

MICHAEL. Why not? Everyone else has.

TANYA (stalking MICHAEL). Tanya is upstairs in bath when friend calls. Go, he say. Go to newstand and purchase *Saturday Review* and read of yourself. Tanya go. Tanya read. Tanya kill!

PHIL. Get in line. I got first dibs on the little weasel.

TANYA (to MICHAEL). For why you do this to Tanya? Is she not your favorite comrade? Does she not get you free tickets for *Porgy and Bess*?

PHIL. Maybe that's why he did it to you.

TANYA. Does little Philomenka want yet *another* nose job? Tanya is more than willing to arrange! (She suddenly notices MARSHALL.) Lenin's ghost! What are you supposed to be? For once, can you not dress like human being?

PHIL. Leave him alone. He can't help it if he only gets lousy jobs!

MARSHALL. What are you calling a lousy job? A part that doesn't deep six while you're playing it?

PHIL. Thanks to *Mr. Literature*, my career is over!

MARSHALL. Again? That's the third time this month!

PHIL. For your information, I landed a part in a play today. On Broadway. With Katharine Hepburn. So, zip it!

TANYA. *You* . . . you are in play with Ekaterina Hepburnova? What you do, kiss-kiss the entire agency?

PHIL (to MICHAEL). Are you just going to let her stand there and talk like that to me?

MICHAEL. I didn't know I was still in the room, let alone the conversation!

TANYA. Why you ask *him* for help — he who write terrible things about Tanya, many of which she does not yet understand. But, when she do . . .

MARSHALL. Put a sock in it, Tanya. Most of what he wrote about you was true.

PHIL. Great. The voice of reason from a man dressed like Tyrone Power in *Blood and Sand*. (This sets off a battle royal, with PHIL alternately siding with TANYA or MARSHALL, whoever is winning.)

MICHAEL (sinking into despair as the noise level increases). I would like to say something here. I really would. No, honestly. I've got something to . . . *hold it*! (ALL freeze.) But I don't have the nerve.

(MIKE appears from the bathroom.)

MIKE. You rang? Nice little party you got going here. They can hear you on Staten Island. By the way, one of Tanya's vocal efforts broke the bathroom mirror.

MICHAEL (to MIKE). How did this get so out of control? When I wrote the article, I never thought — for one minute — that they would react this way.

MIKE. I did. Let's face it. There are quite a few egos in this room. Tanya's alone is the size of Idaho. What did you expect

them to do — thank you for holding them up to the scorn of
New York City and all points west?

MICHAEL.   That's not fair!   I didn't mean to hurt anyone's
feelings! It just seemed like a funny idea!

(MRS. CALDWELL enters from the hallway.)

MRS. CALDWELL.   Like leaving your father *and* mother in
Dayton? And making a public spectacle out of Cindy Evans?
Not that I ever thought she was good enough for you. Were
those your ideas of fun, too?

MIKE.   Take a hike, Mom.   He's got enough problems here.

MRS. CALDWELL.   You know, I never liked these people,
Michael.   Especially the one in the costume.   You were just
being honest in that article.   None of these people has any
talent and someone had to tell them. What right do they have
to complain?

MICHAEL.   Mother, I never said they didn't have any talent.

MRS. CALDWELL.   Well, honestly, darling, you don't really
think they do? At any rate, they're not important, are they?
If they're your friends, how could they turn on you like this?

MIKE.   On the other hand, if you're their friend, what right did
you have to hold them up to ridicule?

MICHAEL.   What ridicule?   Nobody will know that the article
is about them.

MIKE.   *They* know the article is about them. Did you ever stop
to consider how they feel? I think what we've got here is a
bunch of people who feel betrayed . . . and by someone
they cared for. Get the picture?

MICHAEL.   Oh.   (He looks at TANYA, MARSHALL, and
PHIL.) Oh, my God!

MIKE.   Why don't you just tell them how we felt when we wrote
the article? Honesty is usually the best policy. (Aside.) I'm

making myself sick.

MICHAEL. Leave it to me. (TANYA, MARSHALL, and PHIL unfreeze and continue their argument.) *Shut up*! (ALL stop.) Everybody sit down!

PHIL. I don't want to.

MICHAEL. *Sit down*! (ALL sit.) Now can we please try and continue this discussion like rational adults? (Aside.) I think that lets you out, Mother. (MRS. CALDWELL exits in a huff.) I guess I know why you're all mad at me.

PHIL. Aren't *you* the wonder kid!

MICHAEL. Will you please let me get through this, Phil? Okay, the article was selfish and maybe even nasty. But it was the only way I could get through the screams, the bizzarro costumes, and the five-pound chocolate bars from Bloomingdale's!

MARSHALL. And what is that supposed to mean?

MICHAEL. I'm sorry that I hurt your feelings. But it never seems to have occurred to you that I might have feelings, too. No siree, Bob, not ole Michael. He's the straight man who's always around. So what if we disrupt his dates by carrying on like a bunch of clowns? So what if we make fun of his writing? He won't get upset! Do you realize that except for two or three times, you guys have been *on* every time you've set foot in this apartment? It's like this place is a theatre and Michael Caldwell is the built-in audience. So I struck back the only way I knew how. That isn't an article you're so upset about. It's a review. Well, if it makes you want to post the closing notices on our friendship, I am truly sorry. But I'm not like you. I don't have a mental storehouse of one-liners to trot out. I'm just a nice guy from Dayton, Ohio. Maybe it's time I went back there. (There is a moment of silence and MICHAEL crosses to his desk and sits.)

MARSHALL. He certainly got *your* number, Phil. I've been meaning to tell you for two years that your smart remarks about my jobs have been getting on my nerves! Not to mention the *Camille* act we all have to sit through whenever you're out of work!

PHIL. What about all the times I've sat up with *you* after *you've* been canned. Which — not that anyone is keeping score — has been a lot more frequent than the times you've had to bite the bullet with me!

MARSHALL. What bullets? You bite pizzas!

PHIL. Oh, yeah?

MARSHALL. Now there's a scintillating little comeback!

TANYA. The two of you are nudniks! Face facts! One can only be offended by this magazine if one possesses legitimate talent. Philomenka, you are dime a dozen with inflation. Marshall can be replaced by something from grocery store. Only Tanya's legs have true and deep gift. So only Tanya and her legs have right to be offended!

MARSHALL. Tanya, my little Visigoth, I hate to be the one to tell you, but the ability to sit down the way you do does not make you the next Martha Graham.

PHIL. Actually, it doesn't even make you the last Martha Graham. Can't you just schlep into a room like the rest of the human race just *once*?

MARSHALL. Yeah. Every time you come in, it looks like St. Petersburg in nineteen-o-six. I always expect the Tsar to follow you through the door.

TANYA (to MICHAEL). Are you hearing of how they speak to me? (She throws herself into dramatic grief on the couch.)

MARSHALL. Oh, knock it off. I think what we might be saying here is that Michael has a point.

MICHAEL (smugly). Of course, I did. And I think you've all learned a valuable lesson here tonight. You all have these faults, but because we're friends, we can grow and accept each other in spite of them. These honest talks can be very helpful. Don't you agree?

MIKE. I don't think you want to push this too far.

PHIL. Let me get this straight. You feel that basically we're your friends but, like all humans, we have these annoying little traits.

MICHAEL. Uh, yeah.

PHIL (dangerously sweet). And because you're the Methodist St. Francis of Assisi, you felt it was your responsibility to bring them to our attention. Only you couldn't do it any other way than . . . (She holds up the magazine.) . . . this, because you felt it was the only way you could compete.

MICHAEL (becoming uncomfortable as he sees how the conversation is heading). Something like that.

PHIL. And we're supposed to benefit from what you've done to us and, thereby, grow as individuals.

MICHAEL. Yeah.

PHIL. Thus becoming in the long run, better people. So, instead of being angry, we should be grateful for your tremendous human service, right?

MICHAEL. Yeah! I knew that once you thought about it —

PHIL (roaring). Then why do I feel we're being sandbagged?

MIKE. Well, buddy, nice try. Gotta run. (He exits.)

PHIL. What do you mean, *our* faults? Who do you think you are, Pope Michael?

MARSHALL. There are a few things that *you* do that get up *my* nose. Like that three a.m. typing jag you go on periodically. On those nights when romance is in my apartment, it really cramps my style!

PHIL. How often can that happen! (To MICHAEL.) Let's get down to the heart of the matter. For someone who has elevated bland to a lifestyle, you sure throw a lot of rocks!

Did it ever occur to you that we perform around you to keep ourselves awake?

MICHAEL. I just wanted to —

PHIL (cutting MICHAEL off). And people wonder why the midwest has a dull rep! Your personality consists of two moods: indifferent and totally aloof. Nothing ever gets under your skin! You can't even have a decent fight with a person. Not Michael Discipline Caldwell. Oh, no. When you want to get back at people, you have to write it down!

MICHAEL (a little angry). Not all of us are fortunate enough to have a Mediterranean background, Phil!

PHIL. Whoa-ho! Back off, folks! Sarcasm in play!

MICHAEL. Look who's talking!

PHIL. That's right! Slay me with the snappy dialogue! You are *boring* me, Caldwell! Is this the way you used to fight with Cindy?

MARSHALL. Cindy? Who's Cindy?

MICHAEL. You leave *Cindy* out of this!

MARSHALL. Who's Cindy?

PHIL. You haven't gotten the lowdown on Michael's torrid midwestern past? Cindy is *the* woman in his life. They were quite an item. You know, sock hops and Saturday car washes at the church!

MARSHALL. I always wondered what happened to Sandra Dee.

MICHAEL. Cut it out, Phil. I'm really getting annoyed.

PHIL (mimicing MICHAEL). "I'm really getting annoyed." Golly, Michael is peeved.

MARSHALL. Cheese and crackers, Phil, you think so? How can you tell? I don't see any little puffs of smoke coming out of his ears!

MICHAEL. Give me a minute.

PHIL. Are you just going to stand there and take this? No one is giving out any awards for masochism here!

MARSHALL. Let us have it to our faces! We're begging you to! Go ahead! Punch Phil out if you feel like it!

TANYA. Scream, Misha, you feel better!

PHIL. Scream at me! Whatever it is you want to say, scream it at me! (She shakes MICHAEL.) Go ahead and let it out!

MICHAEL (screaming). I love you!

MARSHALL. Oh, my God, I am so *embarrassed*!

PHIL. What did you say?

MICHAEL. Read my lips. I love you. What part don't you understand? I, subject pronoun. Love, active verb. You, direct object. Aren't you the one who dated the English professor?

TANYA. What kind of fight is this? You are supposed to say something *mean*, Misha!

MARSHALL. I think it's time we did that fast samba out to the hall, Tanya.

TANYA. You are crazy! This is best part!

MARSHALL. For them, not for us. (He pushes TANYA toward the door.) Come one. (To PHIL and MICHAEL, who just stare at each other in shock.) We'll let ourselves out. No, honestly, don't make a fuss. We had a lovely time. Let's do it again soon. Say, in twenty years? Nighty-night!

TANYA (at the door). But Tanya wants to stay! (MARSHALL jerks her through the doorway.) Kiss-kiss!

PHIL (after a pause). Well, what do you want me to say?

MICHAEL. I love you, Michael?

PHIL. We'll get to that. First, let's talk about your concept of courtship. What gave you the idea that the way to my heart was humiliating me in a national magazine? Or that telling me you're in love with me in front of a roomfull of people was the kosher way to handle this? What's next? Are you going to hit me over the head and drag me into your cave?

MICHAEL. You were telling me to be more assertive.

PHIL. I said assertive, not Neanderthal!

MICHAEL. Do you love me or not? (A pause.) Do you like me? (A long pause.) Can you tolerate me in the same room?

PHIL. Stop acting like an idiot. We've got problems here. (She paces.) Point one. I love you, too. (MICHAEL beams.) No, no, no. Don't get carried away. And stop looking at me like that! Point two. We have *nothing* in common.

MICHAEL. We're in love with each other, aren't we?

PHIL. I mean important things!

MICHAEL. What could be more important?

PHIL. I don't know. Give me a minute! Okay. What do you like better, pastrami or salami?

MICHAEL. Pastrami.

PHIL (looking at MICHAEL). Who do you like better, Frank Sinatra or Tony Bennett?

MICHAEL. Tony Bennett, but I don't see . . .

PHIL. Shut up! Alright. Here's the clincher. Are you ready?

MICHAEL. I guess.

PHIL. In the unlikely event that we *do* work this out, what would your choice be for the name of our first-born son?

MICHAEL. Mario.

PHIL. Are you willing to put that in writing?

MICHAEL (moving to PHIL). I am willing to do anything that will stop this conversation. Even this. (He kisses PHIL.)

PHIL (breaking). I still think . . .

MICHAEL (kissing PHIL again). You really do talk too much!

CURTAIN

PRODUCTION NOTES

Apartment 5C of the Adolph Zuckerman Home for Artistes isn't much. There is a ramshackle couch with two end tables at C. A desk and chair are R. There is a small kitchenette UL. A door UC leads to the hall. A door UR goes to the bathroom. A door DL leads to the bedroom.

DIRECTOR'S NOTES

DIRECTOR'S NOTES

DIRECTOR'S NOTES

DIRECTOR'S NOTES

DIRECTOR'S NOTES

DIRECTOR'S NOTES